TRUE

CONFESSIONS

OF A

HOUSEHUSBAND,

ALMOST!

C. EARL WEBER I

ISBN: 978-0-9978711-1-1

Printed by Createspace, An Amazon.com Company

DEDICATION

This book is dedicated to my wife who, for over 51 years, has given me love and devotion. She has encouraged me to write about our family, my attempt at performing household duties, and the joys and experiences we have enjoyed together.

TABLE OF CONTENTS

INTRODUCTION

This book, although mostly fiction, does try to bring out some of the problems brought about when the economy dictates that jobs are curtailed, or eliminated, in the workforce. Often, husbands are required to take up the slack on the home front as wives enter or re-enter the job market in place of their husbands. Only some of the episodes are true, but all of them have occurred or have the potential to occur.

It is an impossible task to replace a woman in her own home, but some husbands have tried, unsuccessfully, over the years in their endeavor to take over those impossible duties.

The chapters in this book attempt to bring some humor and levity to the real and imagined problems facing husbands who find themselves taking over household duties previously performed by wives.

x

Chapter 1

Baptism of a Househusband

I have never found out where the term "Househusband" came from. I surmise that my explanation will be as good as any I have thus encountered. I would imagine that the term came about during the 1980s when so many husbands were eliminated from the workforce.

In my mind, a Househusband is a man who has worked and, upon being eliminated from the workforce, has looked for various types of jobs, exhausted his unemployment compensation, tried selling real estate, then reluctantly held the door open for his wife to go to work, while he kisses her as she leaves each day.

Fortunately, for many families, the wife has a marketable skill that can be used to support the family while the husband attempts to take on duties of a housewife; hence the term "Househusband."

On the surface, this is a noble gesture and extremely noble on the wife's part. How nice that the wife has agreed to return to the workforce while the husband has consented to clean the house, wash the clothes, maintain the yard, do the shopping, cook the meals, clean the kitchen, water the dog, and the thousands of other jobs normally done by the housewife. This sounds like an excellent trade-off for the duties of the home and the workplace. But that is not exactly the way things work out. The male workplace is usually made up of many four-letter words that are not acceptable in the family household. It is necessary for the Househusband to learn a new set of four-letter words like cook, iron, wash and dust.

First of all, the home is the domain of the wife – always has been and always will be. Any intruder, regardless of his intentions or relationship, will not do the job correctly in the eyes of his wife. This is the first obstacle that I, as a Househusband, had to overcome. There are three ways of doing a job around the house: the right way, the wrong way, and the wife's way. This is the kindergarten, the genesis, the advent, the Alpha, the only way I can get off on the right foot.

It is the dawning of a new era. Commencement exercises begin the first afternoon the wife returns home. The garbage cans are not in and the garage has not been swept. I did not stack the dishwasher correctly, the furniture has not been dusted, the bed has not been properly made, and an endless list of jobs has been done improperly or not at all. After this GI inspection, then I really get the lowdown on what I failed to do, the wife's way. I always thought that a husband was someone who took out the trash and gave the impression that he just cleaned the whole house.

Never mind the fact that I painted three rooms, answered countless phone solicitations, washed the car, dug up a tree, cleaned the air conditioner filters, and fell asleep on the noon news. Tomorrow will be a different day and I will know just what pleases the working wife.

The next day, I wake up bright and early, see the wife off to work, and start on my day to please her upon her return. But first, the morning paper from the day before catches my eye and I attempt to peruse its contents. Only thing is, my chair is so comfortable that I fall asleep and time goes by so fast that it's time to watch the noon news.

Wife arrival time approaches and I realize that nothing has been done so I move a chair, a vase, rearrange the newspaper just in time to open the door for the Missus. Greetings are exchanged and she runs to the bathroom. Upon emerging from the room of rest, she takes a quick glance around the house and is amazed at the amount of work I have accomplished since I followed her instructions. Now is the time for me to reveal how tired I am and that it would be a wonderful night to go out to dinner with her.

So, off we go to dinner, Househusband driving. I am reminded that I am over the speed limit, took the wrong street, then was directed to a restaurant not exactly my idea of the right choice but, nevertheless, one that we both like.

After being seated, it's time to order and the waiter is standing with pad and pencil at the ready. Wifey is really not too hungry. She and some of the girls went out for a quick bite at lunchtime and she's still full. Never mind that I slept through lunch and I am starving.

My eyes are commanded to shift from the entrees to the salads and I compromise on something I really don't want, since my attention has been diverted to the left side of the menu, away from the better and tastier right side. She orders a salad for herself and a salad for me.

Over dinner I discuss my day with her, only I first have to hear about her day in the workplace. It was horrible. Gloria was having her period and upset everyone. Her boss had had an argument with his wife and was taking it out on everyone else in the office. The air conditioner was not working and the coffee was too strong. The typewriter ribbon had to be changed and it took her all morning to clean up her mess. She ruined her dress from the smudge of the ink from her typewriter ribbon. Sally was caught smoking in the ladies room and filed a grievance when she was reported to management by Betty. Those two have been feuding since day one. During their lunch hour, everyone had a new recipe to discuss so the recipes were exchanged and, of course, Claudia, as usual, disagreed with everyone else and voiced her opinion "ad infinitum."

After the evening news from the work pen, and within the same breath, she asks me how my day was. Did I watch her soaps?

After that question, I am at a loss as to which soap she watches. I ask, trying to show some intelligence, which one, "The White and the Wicked," "The Black and the Beautiful," or "The Fat and the Forgotten"?

She downs her salad in Olympic record time, reaches over to my plate, and picks out the most succulent bite I have been reserving for that most desirable bite of the meal; and, there before my eyes, consumes it and looks around for another one. By now she's full and can't eat another bite. In the meantime, she has eaten the last two loaves of French bread from the bread basket. She then turns to me and says, "Dear, don't you think you've had enough? We can take the rest home and I can bring it for lunch tomorrow."

I then fill up on the water, eye my leftovers being scraped into the "go plate," salivate like Pavlov's dog, and cheerfully lie about the wonderful meal I had and how much I enjoyed it.

Just after I turn off the lights, I ask myself the question, "Do liars deserve a goodnight kiss?" Never mind. I have the headache.

Chapter 2

Add It to My List

One of the first things that I, as a Househusband, learned to do was to make a list of "honey dos." Never mind the fact that I will never get to the end; I need something to show that I have made an attempt at accomplishing my jobs. By scratching off the items as I do each job, it gives me the feeling that I am gaining on it.

I make my list at night for the next day. I then sleep on it that night. The morning brings a new list that my wife insists must be done today. I look at it and start planning. The list includes washing the outside of the house, doing the banking, picking up the groceries, standing in line at the post office, calling the 1 800 number 14 times before I finally get through, cooking dinner, repainting the hallway and, if I get time, making a cake for the bridge game Friday night.

I look at my list, then at hers, and decide that the washing must be done. The dog has to go to the vet, and then I discover a leak in the kitchen sink. What to do first? Get a cup of coffee, get the paper and have my rest before starting. The job naturally requires a trip to the hardware store where I run into a golfing buddy. We brag about the game we should have shot rather than the game we actually shot. Then, back home to the kitchen where I discover I forgot the main washer for the sink trap. I return to the hardware store for the second time. I return home and realize I need plumber's putty. This necessitates a third trip to the hardware store.

By this time, the clerk in the plumbing section tries to hide from me so that he does not have to listen to my problem again. Then, back to my kitchen job and, just as soon as I have my hands full of plumber's putty, the phone rings.

No, I am not interested in having someone come out to give me a price on siding for the house.

There must be some wifely intuition that takes place after these phone calls, for when I get to the best part of the nightly news, my wife asks me to call the siding company for estimates on siding for the house. Put that on my list for tomorrow.

Quitting time at the office arrives, wife gets home, the kitchen is a mess and she's starving. Tonight she will have her choice of "Riscaldato," (Italian for leftovers), "Nokori Mono," (Japanese for leftovers), "Rechauffers," (French for leftovers), or Jambalaya, (regular American leftovers). By that time, all I am interested in is finishing up the plumbing job, cleaning the kitchen, and getting ready for tomorrow's list.

Not all days end up with the list being longer at the end of the day. Sometimes, I actually scratch off several items and can see the end. Whoever said a housewife's work is never done should try to get to the end of the Househusband's list.

But it is comforting to know that at the end of the day, both husband and wife sit together, each in their comfortable chair, sip a glass of Chardonnay, discuss what the Househusband failed to finish, and plan for tomorrow's list.

Househusbands, do not despair. You can always take it out on the family dog. Especially if you get to the newspaper before he does.

Chapter 3

Her Family Dog

It all starts out with something on TV that shows how much company a family dog could be. Then, several days later, the conversation begins with several stories about Donna's (real name used to protect the guilty) dog and how much company Donna's dog is at Donna's house. I had hoped the subject would stop at this point.

I began to defend myself and my territory by saying, "No, we don't need a dog." At this point, I just as soon have put a dog on my list because the seed had been planted, the die had been cast, and the dog will make its home in my home very shortly.

Each day brings a new story about Donna and her dogs. A cute little black one. The next day, it's a honey-colored one. Then, the size is reported. The mother is only 4 pounds and daddy is only 3 pounds. Mathematically speaking, I would say that the new dog will weigh somewhere around 3 ½ pounds. Physically speaking, there is no way those two dogs could mate unless platforms are used in the process. Genetically speaking, by averaging the weight of the mother's 4 pounds and daddy's 3 pounds, the baby is expected to be 3 ½ pounds.

One should now expect that we are about ready to acquire a new dog that will weigh about 3 to 4 pounds according to the previous calculations. Maybe we should refigure those numbers and figure on the weight of both parents combined. That is more than likely what will happen.

Eventually, the new dog arrives; small, honey-colored, loves the newspaper and, eventually, adds his expected 3 ½ pounds to his mother's 4 plus his daddy's 3, and ends up weighing 10 ½ pounds. Where did things go wrong? You can't mix physics, mathematics, and genetics and expect to get the desired weight.

I can tell that the new dog's master is my wife. Somehow the dog has gained access to her capacity to add to her list of things to do and that keeps growing like a hole in your sock. The dog soon becomes adept at making its own list. Take me outside. Clean my water bowl. Change the paper. Clean my food bowl. Change the paper. Go to the vet. Change the paper. Play ball with me. Change the paper.

We are constantly urged to recycle our newspaper, but with a dog around the house, how does one get old newspaper to recycle? Is it possible that recycled newspapers might contain residue after the dog uses it?

My wife's dog was most clever when he summed up a much-publicized rape trial recently held in Florida for a member of one of America's most prominent families. His opinion was expressed when he puddled on the picture on the front page of the newspaper article. I was given credit for teaching him a new trick. His actions expressed a more adequate comment on the event than most newspapers' stories did.

Househusbands will learn that when a dog comes to reside at their workplace, they better be prepared for a change of life. Whenever the new member does something right, it's her dog. When the dog does the wrong thing, it's your dog. Her dog does his business outside. My dog does his business inside. Her dog ate his food. My dog ate her slipper. Her dog sleeps most of the night. My dog is crying. I have to go see about my dog. My dog is barking.

"What am I going to do about it?" My dog dug a hole under the fence. Add fixing that to my list of things to do.

Her dog is a lot of company to me during the day. He gets loose, he wets the carpet, he digs in the trash, he pulls out the clothes in the laundry room, and he hides the shoes, chews the cabinets, and reads the newspaper to see what he can do next. My Darling Wife Honey Bun comes home, picks up the dog, hugs him and calls him by all kinds of wordy endearments; then, she looks at me and asks me if I did all the things on my list.

How can I complete the list? The dog got hold of it and, you guessed it, it was too soggy to read.

But a dog is not all that bad. He does give me a chance to repaint the cabinets he chewed up. He gives me the opportunity to change the carpets and replace my favorite chair, slippers, and golf shoes. Having a dog also provides me the opportunity to work on my temper. I really should not fuss at the poor little 10 ½ pound honey-colored mutt. Who knows? He might know a secret method of conversing with his master and will tell all my secrets!

I forgot to mention that the mutt is named Socrates Augustus. He earns his keep by barking at anyone who gets within 50 yards of the house. Once he makes contact with the object of his bark, I could swear that he has found a long lost friend. He commences a greeting appropriate to finding a long lost buddy. He loves children and will chase a baby stroller for blocks. He loves joggers and they will break their stride when he catches their pants legs. Then the jogger has to stop and catch Socrates to return him home.

He loves the neighbor and runs out to greet him whenever he sees him. Socrates even had a friend until one day he thought the neighbor's leg resembled a fire plug. I offered to take his pants to the cleaners but, somehow or other, Socrates was forgiven and the neighbor took care of the cleaning himself.

Socrates loves to play ball, chase, and hide and seek. When the grandchildren come over to visit, they love to hide his ball. I cover his eyes while the grandchildren hide his ball. He then runs around looking for it until he finds it and then repeats his game to the delight of the grandchildren.

When company comes for a visit, Socrates must make his presence known and will demand that he be introduced. He has never met a stranger and believes that the company has come in just to visit with him. He thinks he is really great at making them feel welcomed.

It is necessary for the Househusband to rise at 4AM, tiptoe out to get the paper, and read it before Socrates gets a chance to express his feelings on the day's news. Afterwards, I must put him out so that he can sniff around for the proper place to relieve himself. I am required to wipe his feet with a clean, dry towel so that "Poor Little Socrates" does not track his damp feet on the floor of his play area. I must also be prepared to render a full report to his master once I return to the bedroom.

During his life with us, Socrates has loved to travel and has had his own special seat, bed, and newspaper in our motor coach. We have traveled all over the US and Canada, and Socrates always maintained a passport and necessary dog papers. He particularly enjoyed his own personal bed in a hotel in Nova Scotia. Then, he accompanied his mother on the downtown streets in his mother's special baby carrying sling and enjoyed shoppers who asked to take his picture.

The daily morning report must also be accompanied with a tray containing my wife's Cappuccino, toast, marmalade, napkin, and a verbal report on how I was received by Socrates. I wonder if Donna needs another dog!

Chapter 4

It's Still a Woman's World

If any Househusband doubts that women still have control of the world, forget it. I have proof that they do.

The National Organization of Women (NOW) can say all they want about women's liberation, but I think the time has arrived when all Househusbands will confirm this matter. Just stay at home and answer the phone, read the magazines, watch the TV, or shop the local supermarket. Everything pertaining to the home is oriented towards the woman. We Househusbands don't stand a chance.

To begin with, the population of the world continues to depend on the weaker sex to repopulate, since the stronger sex is weaker than the weaker sex because of the weakness of the stronger sex for the weaker sex. The stronger sex is not strong enough to accomplish this task alone. The weaker sex says yes, no, maybe so, certainly when the time comes for additions to the family.   The weaker sex also has more headaches than the stronger sex. This can be proven if a survey is ever taken. I'm sure scientists are working on ways to reverse this but, so far, we have to be content and let nature continue to take its course.

Phone solicitors always ask for the woman of the house. They never want to talk to the man of the house or the Househusband. Househusbands are smart enough to know that those phone calls will never be passed on to the darling wife upon her return from the work arena. I only add to my work list when I do.

I think I heard about a recent survey by the local mop company revealing that mops weighing 7 to 8 pounds, when wet, are preferred by present day households. That question was asked of the housewife and should have been asked of the Househusband. I found the survey forms at the supermarket and had some printed so that I could influence the survey. I like the heavier mops since they finish the job faster than the lighter, feminine type. Mops still come in ladies sizes of 2 to 4 pounds, have light pastel colors to match the décor of their kitchens, and handles that are so small in circumference that it feels like you are using a pencil for a handle.   Why don't the people who manufacture mops increase the size of the mop, add a larger handle and paint them camouflage colors more appealing to the male users? I think I would be happier using these new types of mops.

Old wool socks make better dust rags than the old undershirts or cloth diapers. This Househusband found this out when I continued to knock over vases, pictures, and treasured items that have to be dusted almost daily. The old sock makes it easier since it is small enough to fit over your hand and not drag its tail behind it. However, watch the commercials and you will notice there is a housewife pushing the products that profess to make it easier to dust with and a joy to do the dusting. That will be the day when they show a Househusband demonstrating a product of his liking!

I finally called the siding company today. They would be happy to come out and give us an estimate for siding on our house. Once they found out our address, they wanted to know when my wife would be home. She had to be home when they came out. Not just the husband, but both the wife and the husband had to be present. I told them that I was old enough to obtain the bids and that I did not need my wife's permission. For some reason, that was the end of the siding item on my "honey do" list.

My job list had an item listed that required me to paint the living room. No sweat. I knew just what to do, how to do it, and had the necessary items to complete the job. The only thing needed was the paint. Still, no sweat. A trip to the paint store could accomplish that little task. I changed clothes, got out the credit card, and started my trip to the paint store. I had everything in order, or so I thought, but upon arrival at the store, I found that I needed a note from my wife stating the color, type of paint, and an affidavit signed by me stating that she had finally decided upon that shade, finish, price, and amount. I, further, had to sign a statement that the information contained was true and correct and that the paint store would not be held liable for the wrong color, shade, finish, or end results upon completion of the job.

The legal document was then "faxed" to her office, notarized, and returned with five copies: one to be filed at the paint store, one for the manufacturer, one for the clerk of court, one copy to be sent to the Bureau of Vital Statistics, and the last one to be thrown away. I never did get my copy. I forgot to turn on the fax machine before I left home.

I finally did get the paint after a check with VISA and more affidavits stating that I had permission from my wife to use the credit card. The clerk was also kind enough to furnish me with a new paint chart for my next job.

Homecoming that afternoon was most eventful. Socrates had gotten loose in the neighborhood, the garage door was open for all the neighbors to see its disaster, the siding company was calling to find out when my wife would be home, and my dinner was burning on the stove.

The new paint chart was studied and tomorrow's list was topped with, "return the paint and see if you can exchange for a different shade and finish."

Two weeks later, I was still trying to clean up the paint spots from the floor and waiting for the paint to obtain the desired finish. I have yet to learn flat from gloss, semi-gloss, satin from dull, and why I should have used a nylon brush instead of a natural bristle one.

My wife teaches nursing and she's good at it. But, somewhere in the back of my mind, I think she would have made an excellent prosecuting attorney. She always comes up with more questions than any dedicated Househusband can think of. My list can include a trip to the store for a single item. When I purchase that item and return home with it, she might ask if there were other items in a larger container, was it cheaper in another brand, did the other brand contain less fat per ounce, couldn't I find one with a different expiration date on it. I think she has even asked if it was low sodium and low cholesterol.

My "to do" list included an item for me to call and find out the price of theater tickets. I did an excellent job by remembering to call and get the price. I was proud of myself. I did something right. Right? Wrong! Why didn't I think to ask if they were on the main floor or the balcony? Does the price include validated parking in the lot next door? Can we use the discount coupon from the local paper to purchase tickets? Did I get her permission to use the VISA card?

I don't even attempt to say that I will call again tomorrow and get all these questions answered. If I do get all the answers, I will be presented with a new list that I should have known needed answers.

I remember the golden rule, Househusbands: "I have lived with my wife for so many years that, by now, I should know just what she is thinking." She can read my mind; why can't I read hers?

Chapter 5

How Not to Clean House

Today is the day this faithful Househusband has set aside to clean the house. That tops my two page "to do" list. The first thing I do is read the list, then, I go out to get the paper.

Good news and bad news. I beat Socrates to the paper. However, the rain has soaked it so that it is totally unreadable. Not even recyclable. So, back to the "honey do" list that the dog has been trained, by its master, not to render useless.

I walk into the first room. I survey the situation and debate with myself where to start. I start by picking up the clothes to determine if they should be hung up or placed in the dirty clothes hamper. The hamper is full so I must start a load of washing. Then, I have to take the dry cleaning clothes to the cleaners.

A quick look at the news, then back to the "honey do" list. Make the bed, pick up the dirty coffee tray and return it to the kitchen. The kitchen needs cleaning so I start by unloading the dishwasher from the night before, and then reload the dishwasher with the breakfast dishes. Whoever described the dishwasher as a labor saving device? Clean dishes are put away, dirty dishes are stacked, counters wiped, Socrates is put out, and now it's time to mop the kitchen floor.

By now, it is time to consult the list for my banking duties, grocery shopping, cleaners, and check on the book at the library I forgot to get yesterday. I start out doing these little jobs and, finally, after standing in line at the grocery and bank, and waiting for the computer to be fixed at the library, I head home. It is also pushing 11AM by this time and I must consider lunch.

I reheat the gourmet leftovers from last night and turn on the news only to hear that the news has been preempted by the soaps from yesterday since yesterday's soaps were preempted by the news. I suffer through the first part of the "Have and the Haves Not," but fall asleep during the last part. My nap is over when the lady on the screen says, "And that's today's news. We'll see you at this same time tomorrow."

At this point, I figure that all news must have been postponed for today and I'll have the same chance to experience these activities tomorrow.

All of a sudden, I am reminded of the cleaning job I started, the clothes in the washer, and Socrates is outside! What to do first? Run after Socrates, get him in, give him a snack, throw the clothes in the dryer, get out the pastel colored pencil thin mop, mop the kitchen floor, run upstairs and start my cleaning. I make the bed, clean the bathrooms, fix the leaky faucet, dust the furniture, vacuum the carpets, re-dust after emptying the cleaner bag, relax and admire my progress.

I move on to the next room, repeat the entire cleaning process, rearrange everything in its proper place and move on to the next room. I marvel at my efficiency and ability to get things in order so fast. Yet, I fail to realize how short-lived these accomplishments are. I'll have a chance to do it all over again tomorrow.

I turn on the news. A bolt of lightning strikes me that I have given no thought or energy to dinner. I rush downstairs, look in the refrigerator and start pulling out tonight's dinner. I find a casserole dish with meatballs from last week. That's a start. What are the other "pastabilities?" That's it! Pasta. I boil the water, throw in the pasta, look for the pasta sauce and, all of a sudden, I realize that I am on the road to becoming a "Gourmet Short Order Chef." I also learn how to cook pasta without it boiling over.

I interrupt my culinary efforts to clean the stove of the pasta juice that has boiled over. Then, I return to the task I left, combine the pasta, meatballs, grate the cheese, find some bread crumbs, put it into the oven and wait. And wait! And wait!

I'll wait until eternity unless I turn on the oven. To make up for lost time, and to be sure I have the dinner ready when the "Warden" (lovely wife) gets home, I turn up the oven to about 500º. This time, I do not have to wait long. My "Culinary Creation" has boiled over, is burning in the oven, the smoke alarm has gone off, Socrates has to be let outside and, of course, the phone rings and the nice lady asks if I would like to have someone come out and give me a price on siding.

The creator of the "honey do" list arrives and is unable to get her car in the garage. Someone (me) has used my car and parked it in the middle and she cannot get hers in the garage. You might know it is raining, I did not put her umbrella in her car, and she gets wet when she has to walk in the rain from her car.

After the third glass of wine, Chablis today, things become more bearable and the two of us sit down to discuss each other's day. I must then defend myself as to why the two page list is still ¾ full. No excuses tolerated. Cancel tomorrow's golf game and get busy on the list.

Did I get to watch her soaps today? What soaps? I must remember to tape her soaps, "The Sad and the Sassy," tomorrow. I answer in the affirmative that I will remember.

Later in the evening, I remember the clothes in the dryer and rush down to remove them for folding. I also forgot to clean the kitchen, fix the coffee pot for in the morning, water the dog, mop the kitchen, and prepare my list for tomorrow.

After finally collapsing in bed for the night, I forgot to bring up the glass of water for the night tray, so off I must go to do this one last chore. While I am downstairs, Socrates has to go out. After barking at the moon for 15 minutes, he finally decides that he, too, must call it a day. I've learned, at this point, that too much housework can kill you.

By the time I get back upstairs, I find the light has been turned off and the television has been shut down for the night.

Never mind! I have the headache again.

Chapter 6

Time to Organize

I soon realized that something was missing from my daily life. The problem was what to do about it. I tried the internet to see if something could be done to improve my lot but nothing jumped out at me. Somewhere out there in the world, I knew that there would be others who fit into the same category as me.

Once again, the internet gave me no clues as to who might be having the same problems with being a Househusband as I was having. What could be done to alleviate the situation and, at the same time, be of help to man and mankind? How could I help myself and, at the same time, help others?

The idea came to me one day while I was using my pink handle light weight mop. It was like an electrical shock that rose like lightning that almost knocked me off my feet. I had to sit to

27

recuperate, have a cup of coffee, take a short nap, and set my course to implement my new idea.

I first contacted a local CIO organization to solicit their help. I was turned down so fast that I almost gave up completely on the idea. I felt that if I did not follow my instincts, continue with my idea, I would be leaving thousands of Househusbands abandoned to the rules and regulations pertaining to their future problems as Househusbands.

I tried contacting the AFL, IRS, FEMA, CIS, FBI, CIVIL AIR PATROL, BSA, ROTC, and several other organizations but those contacted refused to offer any help. They all agreed that something should be done and encouraged me to continue, albeit, without their help. They also referred me to the TSA. I contacted them but their main concern was that they be allowed to inspect all activities according to their own rules.

The Teachers' Union wanted to get into the act but we felt that competition would be too great with the head of the household. Also, the intent was to organize against, not with, the wives. So, more problems were encountered in my endeavor to organize the Househusbands into a group of frustrated Househusbands.

After so many rejections by organized groups, the idea came to me to organize our group into one that would encompass all of us and serve as a vehicle to assist us in our endeavor. We could form our own support organization.

Voilà! Henceforth, Househusbands would unite and form their own support group. This group would be known as the BATTERED AND ABUSED HUSBANDS CLUB (BAHC). Now, we could continue with our plans to unite.

The first order of business was to discuss what bylaws were needed to become a viable and progressive organization. We contacted all the Househusbands we knew and were amazed at how cooperative and enthusiastic they were. It soon was apparent that husbands in the working force wanted membership in the BAHC so the bylaws were amended to accommodate them. We all felt that too much housework could make you croak.

We now needed a place to assemble for our business meetings. The first thought that came to our minds was to meet at someone's home but the wives refused this request. We next tried the church halls to no avail. Banks turned us down, private clubs joined in with their refusals, and the weather refused to let up so that we could use the city park.

The membership increased like wildfire. We were overwhelmed with so many applications that more problems were created than were solved. We just could not handle the requests for joining the BAHC. We needed help. Who could we turn to? We had no funds, requests for bank loans were turned down, and we were stymied in our efforts. We were at a roadblock. Unable to move forward, we then turned to the only possible means of obtaining help.

We begged our wives to allow us to meet in a member's home, but this suggestion was met with deaf ears. "No indeed" would they allow us to use their homes for BAHC meetings. Our request for club business was turned down flat!

Their reply to their refusal was their own organization, the BATTERED AND ABUSED WIVES CLUB (BAWC). They held closed meetings in their homes so we were not able to attend as members of BAHC.

That movement brought a death-dealing blow to the BAHC so we had to go underground. We agreed to meet every Monday night; the time and place would be announced at a later date. However, we failed in our efforts to obtain a kitchen pass to attend the meetings so our meetings were, and are, limited to casual meetings when the members of BAHC encounter each other by chance. At this point, we even tried casual meetings at the supermarkets but management made it absolutely clear that that would be a violation of their policy. The BAWC threatened boycott of their stores.

We still look forward to a bright future for the club and considerable interest continues to be shown by present and potential members. In the meantime, the BAHC continues to flourish.

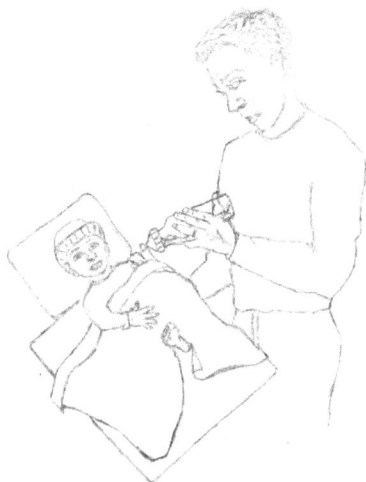

Chapter 7

Children, to Have or to Have Not

The decision to have children or not to have children in a marriage is usually a subject that is discussed by both partners prior to and after the wedding. Not all newlyweds are in agreement that they should procreate and add to the problems of world population. Likewise, many parents who have had children question their decision during the children's growth into adulthood.

This is always a question that comes up in a marriage, but one that a Househusband does not have to worry about. The housewife usually has the last word in this matter. Some Househusbands have the last word; some have not. The correct answer is always, "yes, Dear."

I belong to the have nots when it comes to children. It was not always this way. I had; now, I have not. I still have, but I have not. What I mean is that those I did have, I have not the obligation of providing bed and board, bath, meals, car, insurance, shelter, tuition, and free kitchen privileges I once was required to provide.

They are gone, but not forgotten. It is impossible to forget them. They still return, but now they bring "theirs" with them. I still provide the food, shelter for short periods of time, and other indexes of services, but those services are referred to as babysitting. After all, when they return home, your children are returning to the place of their childhood and they play the part. They expect to be waited on, hand and foot. They cannot remember to pick up behind themselves, and their children become your children once they enter the premises.

They never changed diapers when they were home, so why should they start now? Meals were prepared and served by Mom and still are. Visiting children seem to have the idea that child management becomes the responsibility of Grandparents once they cross the threshold of Grandmother's house. And, of course, the Grandparents are only too happy to oblige since this is the only time they seem to get quality time with the grandchildren.

I am just waiting for the day when Househusbands and Housewives are offered degrees equal to, or exceeding, those offered in academic circles. I feel that we would qualify to enter into the postgraduate curriculum without further prerequisites.

My duties as a Househusband no longer include the responsibilities of children in the household. The walls and halls, table and chairs, and closets and cars are no longer hosts to the eighteen feet that once stood ready for their demands. Our nine children taxed the structural capacity of the house, the financial limits of the bank account, and the mental capacity of their parents. They continue to cause us to live in fear that they will return home for their version of continuing education.

We live in fear that they will someday return home. Only this time, they will have their own children with them. Once they do return, their children will then become our children. This is enough to keep us awake at night and guard the entrances during the day. The worst-case scenario would be for all nine children to return with all forty-five of the grandchildren plus their spouses.

I know that somewhere, someplace, there is a travel agency that offers refuge to Grandparents caught up in that predicament.

Grandchildren are, and always will be, welcomed in our household. If you doubt my sincerity, watch how I clean up for them before their arrival, after they leave, while they are here, between meals, during meals, after meals, and even while they are sleeping. I want them to experience a germ-free environment, a dust-free room, nutritious food, and adequate programs on television. Add to that the latest computer games, toys, DVDs, CDs and discs of all the latest children's movies, rental privileges at the video store, and an inexhaustible supply of junk food for their welfare and enjoyment while visiting.

Also, they expect me to be prepared to extend cash grants to those who did not have time to cash a check before leaving home and need as little as fifty or seventy-five dollars just for the afternoon. These grants are equal to the grants that we make to third world countries. The money is granted but never repaid. The main provision of these grants is that I grant them the privilege of my money and the permission for not ever seeing it again.

Visiting children are most happy to let me play with their children while they go shopping. They are quick to tell me that they will be back within the hour, and I can proceed with my own nap; but, just listen for the baby while it sleeps. They never mention which hour.

Once I recover my composure, the parent and Grandmother are out of the house and gone before I have time to say, "I refuse."

The sleeping child, sensing that the parent is no longer at its beck and yell, then mysteriously wakes from its deep sleep and proceeds to demonstrate its various methods of gaining one's attention. The child's performance could be nominated for an Oscar if I had the time to video the action.

There is absolutely no way I can get the child to give in to the fact that I am in charge and I will not tolerate its unacceptable behavior. My suggestion that the child stop this behavior is answered with an odor emitting from its diaper that would qualify as poison gas for a chemical warfare drill. The child has performed encopresis and I am the only one home to remedy the situation.

Once that is done, the yelping should have ceased. Right? Wrong! Now I must look around for something to feed the little darling. Only thing is, Mother forgot to fix the formula and did not tell me the proper mixture. No wonder, she is breastfeeding.

Seven different mixings and forty-eight minutes later, I hit upon the combination that seems to please the little one and I plug up the yap that is causing the neighbors to close their windows to tone down the sound. I encourage the little one to gulp down the contents so that I can get back to my nap.

Another few minutes and I just know that I will have the baby fed, dry, and asleep; then, the Househusband Grandfather Babysitter will be free. Except for the fact that the wet one has to be changed for a dry one!

Now, the baby is wide awake and wanting to play. So I play, and play and play some more till it's time for another bottle.

No problem! I know the formula. I get the formula. I feed the formula. Baby now returns to the crib and falls fast asleep within the first few minutes. Now, I am able to spend quality time with myself – at least for the next three minutes. The girls then return, after being gone for four hours, with their arms loaded with their shopping items and are marveled that their little one has slept during the entire time that they have been shopping. Househusband Grandfather Babysitter did an excellent job and they just knew that I would have no trouble with the little one.

No chance for me to get in my version! A sound has emitted from the little darling and both run to see about taking it into their arms for cuddling time and to tell baby what a wonderful child it has been. "You see, Paw Paw; I knew you would have no trouble taking care of the little one."

I realize at the next feeding, too late, that I did not give the little darling baby formula, but I gave it the eggnog that Grandmother was saving for her bridge party tomorrow night.

Baby also lets me know that the formula I gave it is causing problems such as crying, stomach pains, gaseous explosions, diarrhea, stares from Mother and Grandmother, and threats that I will be reported to the SPCA for child abuse. Strange noises begin to be emitted from the little one as Grandfather gets the blame and is told to apologize and then ordered to go and unload the car.

The child sleeps all night for the first time since its birth. The eggnog seemed to do the trick.

I tell everyone this at the breakfast table the next morning and suggest that maybe baby is not getting enough nutrition from the formula. I am convinced that the child is hungry.

I am attacked from all sides, refused a second cup of coffee, refused butter and jelly for my toast, ignored, deserted by all the others at the table, left to clean up the table, do the dishes, mop the floor, and then take Socrates for a watering.

I feel down and out. Rejected. Unloved. An abuser. Abused. Neglected. Not fit to be left alone with the poor little one. How dare I feed infant eggnog instead of formula! My home will never again be the same. I think of leaving for a foreign country. I start packing my suitcase. I put my bag in the car trunk. Tonight will be the night. Everything is all set. All I have to do is just wait until dark. The countdown has begun. I am sitting in my chair for just one last time, contemplating my failure as a Househusband, Father, Grandfather, Great Grandfather, babysitter and a man. I feel as low as a person can get. I am on the verge of tears.

I am approached by two vaguely familiar figures. One is my daughter, the other is her Mother. I am greeted by mellifluous sounds and words from them and I wonder if the barometric pressure has fallen and caused some disturbance in their bodily functions.

The bomb is then dropped. "Honey, will you stay with the baby while we go shopping for about an hour? We know you will have no trouble."

Chapter 8

Ideas and Opinions

Househusbands are not permitted to have ideas. Neither are they allowed to have opinions on anything, unless they have the same opinions as the commanding officer.

I had an idea some years ago that I would wallpaper the washroom. I did not need to purchase any materials since we had enough wallpaper covering left over from a previous job. I was real pleased with myself, for I had the bright idea of invoking life into the lifeless walls and marveled at the fact of my contemplated ingenuity.

One morning, just after a routine departure by my wife, I set out upon my task. Within a short period of time, I progressed past the halfway mark long before the return of the "lady of the house." I was very proud of my work and completed the job before her arrival time. The room looked wonderful, and all my tools were cleaned and put away before Wife came home.

The usual greetings varied and even Socrates was ignored until the strange odor was identified. I was questioned about the strange odor that permeated the house. Not wanting to expose my "escapade for the day" too early, I pretended not to notice any variance from the norm.

She could not rest until the foreign odor was identified. She looked all over the house. Begged for help. Pleaded. Commanded. I was forced to expose the source of the odor. I reluctantly pointed to the washroom and the magnificent job of wallpapering I had done.

Horror of horrors! Why did I do that? Where did I get the paper? Why did I use that particular paper? She was saving it for another project. I should have obtained her permission before doing such a thing. Next time, consult her before undertaking such a project!

After enjoying a silent dinner, I sheepishly offered to clean the kitchen, mop the floor, bathe the dog, change the paper, put out the garbage, fix the coffee pot, and turn down the covers on the bed, hoping that I could occupy my usual place in it for the night.

While serving my sentence and keeping busy with my chores, the phone rang. I knew better than to think that it was a call for me. I had to answer it, bring the portable phone to "Mother Superior," turn down the TV, and return to my penal duties.

I could not help but overhear parts of the phone conversation and I was almost floored when I overheard the comments about the wallpapering job. I could not believe what I was actually hearing. Never in my wildest dreams did I ever think that I would actually hear what was being said on the phone.

She said to the person on the phone, "You should see how nice my washroom looks. I had my Househusband wallpaper the room and it looks marvelous. I picked out this paper that just matched everything in the room and I made him take his time to do a good job. I have such wonderful ideas!"

I could not believe that I was hearing such comments from the person who had just castigated me for the audacity of doing such a thing without her permission. I waited until the phone call was finished, then I made my presence available so that I just might hear a change of heart from my permanent roommate. It never came.

I did vow and declare, at that point, that if I ever got another idea, I would throw out hints about it and wait for it to be her idea. This seemed to be a good idea, but I was forced into taking a course in psychology. I will have to learn how to give her an idea about what my idea is. That way, it will be her idea and not mine.

Now that I have mastered this feat, things are going better around the house and she has furnished me with an adequate supply of ideas.

Opinions work very much the same way. I am not allowed to express an opinion unless my opinion is the same opinion as the "lady of the house."

I am never allowed to choose the color of a room. If I want it white, I must say I want it red. If I want the carpet to be blue, I must say green. If I feel cold, I must complain about being hot. I have learned to ask before expressing my feelings or desires.

"Are we hungry yet?"

"Am I hot or cold tonight?"

"Do I want to watch the football game or do I want to watch 'Dine Nasty'?"

I feel that I have a choice. The only condition is that my choice better be her choice. What other choice do I have?

I have this bit of advice for Househusbands who are Househusbands today, might be tomorrow, or see any possibility of becoming one in the future: Never change the color, size, shape, shade, finish, position, locale, place, spot, or arrangement of any movable or immovable object without first getting the permission, ideas, approval, sanction, and OK of the final authority. This authority should be in writing, on cassette, videotaped, and filed for future defense should it ever come up for trial.

Remember: ideas and opinions are not permitted within the duties, privileges, or obligations of a Househusband. Some things are better left to a higher authority.

Chapter 9

A Day at Home with a Sick Wife

I thought I was prepared for everything. I had been through hurricanes, power outages, floods, freezes, family, friends, guests, vacations, mother-in-law visits, children, grandchildren, great grandchildren, telephone solicitors, siding salesmen, and other choice crises, but I was not prepared for the day "Mother Superior" woke up too sick to report for work.

I must give credit where credit is due. Many days when she should have stayed home from work, she hauled herself out of bed and went off to work. However, this day was one of those days that she was just not able.

My day started out with a simple request. Something like, "Honey, please get me the thermometer." That was easy enough. Or, so I thought.

"Where is the thermometer?" The Househusband groaned.

While looking for the "fever meter," several other requests followed in rapid succession.

"Please get me some hot tea."

"Call the office."

"Plug in the vaporizer."

"Turn off that light."

"Bring me a piece of toast."

"Call the doctor."

"Get me some more tea."

"Change the bed."

"Pick up those clothes."

"Where is the thermometer?"

I questioned myself again as to where she learned to give all those orders in such rapid succession. This served only to reinforce my thinking that she had served in the military at some time before our marriage. Perhaps it was in the Pentagon, since the orders were issued "military style."

I did a fairly good job of complying with all her immediate requests and was finally ready to start my daily ritual. I put out the dog, got my paper, fixed my tea, and sat down to read the morning news. That was not meant to be. Just as I sat down, some alarm went off and I was summoned to receive additional orders from the "sick one."

I was dictated a list of items that the local drug store should have. I then embarked upon the journey to purchase the desired items. I forgot to remember that the only acceptable medicines were to be in the correct size, milligrams, brands, kilograms, extra strength, dosage, and not the new and improved versions of the listed items.

I returned home, produced my purchases, received instructions for what to return for exchange, returned to the drug store and sought out the items, exactly as listed. The first store was out of the brand name as listed on the list, the second store did not carry that item, and the third store would have that brand that afternoon.

I returned home again, and the momentous decision was made that the item I returned would suffice. So, I retraced my steps and returned to "rebuy" the medicine I had returned. By that time, the clerk knew me and was almost willing to let me take things home on approval.

Upon arrival back home, I was given a new set of orders. The room needed dusting and the bathroom needed cleaning. Next, open the curtains, close the curtains, and get rid of the odor from the cleaning equipment.

The jobs were carried out, along with a few others. I lit a candle and put it on the dresser. I knelt in prayer, silently praying that the sickness would be purged from my sick wife. She seemed impressed by this and I once again began to think about her earlier life, perhaps the Mother Superior in a nun factory.

I was furnished instructions on how to make a soup, what to cook it in, where all the ingredients were, and told that I should begin cooking immediately.

Down to the kitchen I went, charging into the cabinets, digging into the pot pantry, and proceeded to combine the listed ingredients. A call from upstairs caused me to check on the "sick one." More tea, change blankets, and numerous questions as to how I was doing with my list of things to do! Added to the list were requests to water the dog, mop the kitchen, and do the washing; but, don't wash her personal things as she would do them later.

Soup is on, boiling away, and everything seems to be calm for the moment. I try to steal a few minutes to read the paper. I sit in my chair. The alarm goes off and I am summoned to the bedside of the sick once again. I am convinced there is some kind of a signal that is given off once I sit in my chair to relax. It never fails that, just as I sit down, I am immediately requested to jump up and do another job.

Water is needed to take her medicine and she cannot find the remote control for the TV. Of course she can't find it. It's under her pillow.

Not being a medicine man, I am unable to unravel the mystery as to how the "sick one" gets considerably better when it's time for the soaps. She not only feels better, but has decided that I should "revictulate" and has made another list for me. No big hurry but, while I'm out, please pick up some clothes at the cleaners, return this library book, get a paint chart from the hardware store, and hurry home to finish cooking dinner.

Soup is served. Tasted. No salt. I get the salt. No crackers. I get the crackers. The spoon is too small. I get a larger spoon. I learn that I should put carrots, onions, tomatoes, and herbs in the soup. It is not possible that these instructions can be given to me all at once. I must climb the stairs each time an instruction is issued. Next time, add some meat to the soup so that it will be more nutritious.

I followed her list verbatim, as instructed, and then I am told that I should use my own judgment about some things. It's about like playing the lottery. You win some, you lose some. But the majority of the time, you lose.

I am convinced that when nurses get sick, they use up their entire portfolio of patient requests on the poor Househusband. They must obtain pleasure from using all these requests just to get back at those patients who dealt them so much misery over the years. It sure seems as though nurses are taught that when they are sick, they must use every excuse and command in their repertoire to repay those they've nursed over the years!

By mid-afternoon, I have just about given up on reading the morning paper. I feel like I have just finished competing in a triathlon and finally crossed the finish line. The soaps are over and some show about "Wives Win Freedom" has just come on. Today's topic is "Abused Househusbands" and the sick wife is propped up in bed getting new ideas.

I am not allowed to watch this program for fear that I might associate with those who are appearing on the show.

Her voice shatters the silence, summoning me to her bedside once again. I think of the last list and wonder what she could possibly want this time.

She would like to have some attention and requests that I bring Socrates upstairs to visit. She's sure he's lonesome for her. They are happy to see each other. I am sent on additional errands. Socrates needs a toy to play with.

By this time, I figure that my patient has responded to the tender loving care treatment I have given her and I will have my house to myself tomorrow. I light a candle in thanksgiving. Tomorrow, I will read today's paper and tomorrow's paper. My list will not be revised hourly. I look forward to tomorrow and the satisfaction that I did such a marvelous job of nursing without any formal training. I congratulate myself. I even put on a smile. I am comfortable. Day is done.

Then, I hear the voice of the "Mother Superior General" as she softly tells me, "I think I'll stay home tomorrow to make sure I'm well before going back to work."

Chapter 10

Househusband Gets Sick

Sooner or later, or finally, Househusband wakes up one morning with pains in my joints, fever, sore throat, burning eyes, upset stomach, and a few other symptoms that tell me I must have something wrong with my body. I grope around and try to get a little sympathy from my loving wife, nurse, Sergeant, Mother Superior, only to be told to hurry and get her coffee. She is running late this morning.

I try to open my eyelids, reach for the nonexistent crutches, force my swollen feet into my slippers, and tumble down the stairs for the breakfast tray. I feel proud of myself for remembering to include the sugar and cream on the tray, only to learn that I should have included the artificial sugar. I "unclimb" the stairs to look for the artificial sugar and return to the upstairs bedroom with my findings, only to be told that I must return downstairs to reheat the cold coffee.

My return is greeted with a command that I should stay warm, drink plenty of fluids, take the pills that will be left for me, and be sure to take care of the dog so that he will not get sick.

Wifey runs out the door shouting instructions for what I am to do to get myself well, and adds to my list for the day. Her promise to bring me some hot broth before leaving is forgotten, or ignored, when she stops to tell her lovely dog goodbye.

I linger with my pains. I look for the medicines, hunt for the "fever meter," groan, and wait for the hot liquid. Finally, about 11AM, I realize that if I desire liquids of any sort, hot or cold, I better start my safari and hunt them down myself. I will have to wait until quitting time for the next promise.

The phone rings, I answer groggily. My darling wife has called to find out if I put Socrates out for his daily exercise. I try to ask her for something to take, but she has a meeting to go to and must hang up immediately.

About this time, I am convinced that I have PMS (Positive Masculine Sickness). I learn later that PMS means something entirely different. I stay close to my chair. I am amazed that I can sit without having to jump up just as soon as I sit down. No alarm went off. I wrap up in a ball under the cover of my "blankie" and just hope that the world will leave me alone with my aches and pains.

Morning passes. Afternoon passes. Quitting time comes around. I am still feeling too bad to move. I just want to hide under the covers, just to be left alone. But, I still feel that something hot would go a long way towards convincing me that someone, somewhere, cares about me.

Even a call from the siding lady would go a long way assuring me that someone in the world, somewhere, still remembers me.

I hear the door open. Wife enters. She checks on Socrates. She sees me balled up under the "blankie" in my chair. She questions me about how I am feeling. She promises to get me some hot tea. She feeds her dog.

The phone rings. She talks for 27 minutes.

She asks if I need anything else.

I ask for hot tea.

She says I just had some.

I look confused. I wonder if I have that disease called…..I forget the name of that disease.

She starts to fix dinner.

I wait.

Again, the question, "Do you need anything?"

I answer in the affirmative.

I wait.

She plays with the dog!

I wait for a glass of water, hot tea, and hot soup; just anything to nourish my undernourished body.

I wait some more.

I am told that I should get up, move around, and walk a little so that I will not get stiff.

I hobble to the kitchen to fix something for myself. I am told that the kitchen is clean and not to mess it up.

I climb over the mess Socrates had made. I am observed eyeing the dog bowl and warned of the dire consequences if I even dare to touch his bowl….

I am so weak and dehydrated, undernourished, forgotten about, ignored, and underfed that I figure it's just not worth being sick around this house.

I finally make it back up to bed, crawl under the covers, snuggle up to my pillows, close my eyes, and drift off into the arms of Morpheus. All night long, I dream. My dreams are pleasant ones. I dream that I died and had been reincarnated. I have returned home again. Only this time, I am the dog.

Chapter 11

Can You Balance the Checkbook?

This is almost an exercise in futility around our house. Try as we might, it is impossible for the two of us to record our checks in the checkbook when they should be recorded.

The simple answer is I should put in more money than she takes out. That is basic, rudimentary, primary, necessary, and logical. In theory, it is taught in all schools of higher learning. In reality, the subject just as soon be written in Chinese in a computer program designed for household budgets. As long as two people write checks on the same account, that account is bound to be so mixed up that it requires a CPA, a tax lawyer, a mathematician, and sometimes an Egyptologist to interpolate.

To begin with, the checkbook is never in its proper place when you need it. It is either in her purse, her car, her desk, or in the box that has the grocery coupons. My memory is such that I must write things down so that I can remember to accomplish them later. Remember the list? I need the list to tell me where the list is that I must follow. I must also remember to refer to that list as frequently as I can find it.

Since we have more than one bank account, and prudence dictates that all households should have, I must remember into which account I must deposit paychecks, and from which account I must write checks to pay bills. This is a matter that must not be taken lightly. The confusion increases proportionately to the number of accounts I keep. No matter what I do, I am bound to get deposits and withdrawals confused and scrambled, leaving both of us frustrated, baffled, disconcerted, overdrawn, and ready to accuse the bank of tampering with our accounts.

After many years of banking, I still have trouble remembering the difference between credits and debits. I am more familiar with NSF. It's about like port and starboard. You must develop a system to remember their meanings.

The bank statement is bulging with checks when it is returned from the bank. I am amazed that so many checks have been written during the past month. As I look over the canceled checks, I start remembering the checks I wrote and failed to record, my list of things I failed to consult, and then vow to record all future checks immediately after writing them.

I retrieve the checkbook, check the stubs, match the checks, and then I begin to record the unrecorded ones. It is then that I realize that we do not have on deposit what I thought we had on deposit. I wonder if checking accounts are feeding upon themselves, eating up our deposits, nibbling away at the balance I thought we had.

The two guilty check writers sit down together and attempt to reconstruct a true and correct bank balance. This is when I learn that all calculators are not created equal. The totals do not match. The decimal point is off. My answers with hers become like milk and cookies; they never come out even.

It is always easy to know when someone has made a mistake. The guilty party, usually me, remembers something that must be taken care of immediately. By the time the guilty one returns, the mistake has been taken care of and forgotten about. Now I know what to do when I am about to get caught in a mistake. Leave!

I think every household should set forth rules and regulations to govern family checking accounts. Some of those rules should be as follows:

1. Never assume the balance in the checkbook is correct.
2. Always start in the last place to look for the checkbook. That is where you always find it.
3. No two calculators are created equal.
4. Never admit that you might be wrong.
5. Always accuse the bank of making a mistake.
6. Do not record deposits. It only increases the balance.
7. Hide your checkbook in different places. It confuses the enemy and you will write fewer checks.
8. Leave blank spaces in your checkbook. That way, you can always go back and record forgotten checks.
9. When in doubt, accuse your partner of the mistake.
10. To avoid mistakes, have only one authorized signature. Hers.

Mother Superior concurs only on number 10 of the above rules and regulations. Henceforth, this household and this Househusband will have only pocket change at his disposal.

Chapter 12

Never Mind the Name,
What Is Your Number?

We are given numbers for everything we do, everything we own, and every account that has anything to do with money, size, and shape.

I recently went to the bank to complain about my balance. Nobody asked me for my name, just my number. I told them that when I opened my account, I gave them my name. They gave me a number. I remember my name, they should remember my number.

Yesterday, my list included a number of items that were nothing but numbers. I was instructed to pay account 00356982 before 5-21-2016 so that we could enjoy the discount of $3.22 on the amount of $46.21.

I began looking for account 00356982 and realized I was looking for the electric bill. Then, I had to find the Social Security number for my wife. Unable to find it, I called 396 7285 to talk to her but she was busy and could not answer her page. I was given a number to call, 342, and then told to hang up and try later. I called the Social Security Office to get "Mother Superior's" number only to be told that they did not issue Social Security numbers to nuns. They also wanted to know why I was married to a nun.

I then proceeded down my list to the next number. I had to call the bank to discuss a problem with our account. If I wanted to discuss deposits, I had to punch 1, if I wanted a loan punch 2, overdraft punch 3, new account punch 4, safety deposit box punch 5. I was also given a number to punch in if I wanted to conduct my business in English or Spanish. If I wanted to discuss deposits, call back tomorrow. The clerk asked me for my account number and I went through the same routine I had gone through before. I, eventually, found my bank account number and called 396 5432 again and identified myself as 27 5602 1. I was then told that office hours were between 8AM and 5PM and to call back tomorrow.

I learned that all accounts operated on the bi-mummery system and I should become acquainted with the system in order to facilitate any future transactions. I never heard of the bi-mummery system, still do not know what it means, never learned it in school, and my brain is programmed to remember only my address, zip code, telephone number, age, anniversary date, wife's birthday, my children's birthdays, grandchildren's birthdays, great grandchildren's birthdays, and Christmas checks.

I finally found and punched 5, called 393 4589, and told them that I was 614573 and wanted to question why I was charged $148.96 for 4000 gallons of water. They explained to me that 20% was charged for the garbage collection, 30% was for sewerage, and 50% was for water. Additional charges were added to my bill for the indigent who could not afford to pay their own water bills. An additional amount of $4.50 was charged for adjustments to cost, and service charges amounted to $10.25. I had the feeling that I was also buying someone's lunch several times a month, and told them so.

I was informed that I could complain further by calling 393 7413 and pressing 1 if I wanted to discuss service, 2 if I wanted to discuss the amount of the bill, 3 if I was late paying my bill, 4 if I wanted to speak to the manager, or 5 if I forgot what I was calling about. I, eventually, punched 5 only to be told that it was a holiday and to call back tomorrow. They also requested that I punch a certain number for English or Spanish. Since I did not speak Spanish and my English verbiage did not work too well, I asked for French, since I have some knowledge of how to converse in the French language.

I consulted my list. I called 396 2199 and told them I was 646 11 6002 and was calling about Social Security number 964 22 8562 to discuss an error of $97.62 on the check that should have been $26.79. I was told that since today was 2-15-2016, I was 31 days too late and would have to wait until 3-16-2016 to reapply for the corrected amount. I was referred to case worker 568 and told to use a touch tone phone and dial 6 to get 568. Having only a rotary dial phone, I was left waiting until their lunch period was over to have my call answered.

I tried calling 911, but the phone I was using did not have number eleven on it. One of the grandchildren, visiting at the time, showed me how to dial 911 and I was put in touch with the proper number.

I dialed 415 3921 and asked for operator 29 to discuss my debit card account. I explained that my account 4520 359 2241 8, with the expiration date of 4-23-2016, was overcharged $20.00 on 3-21-2016. Operator 29 did not have a name and could not tell me why the extra charge of $20.00 was added to my account. She told me to call back next week and ask for another operator.

I started writing my autobiography last week and I was unaware of the number of numbers on my list. I was born 11-11-1928 at 5:43AM. I was told this by my Mother who was there with me at the time. I presently live at 905 Yellowstone Street, zip code 70006, but plan on moving to the 70001 zip code area soon. You can call me at 1 555 491 7825 between the hours of 6AM and 9PM. I also go by the number 555 10 4012 and presently weigh 20 pounds over the weight I would like to weigh. I am also required to remember the following numbers:

Social Security
Date of Birth
Home Address
Business Address
Home Telephone
Cell Phone
Area Code
Zip Code
Driver's License
License Plate
Hospitalization Insurance
Bank Accounts
PIN Numbers
Navy Serial
Air Force Serial
Veterans Administration
IRA Account
Shoe Size
Pants Size

Shirt Size
Cholesterol Count
Wife's Birthday
Children's Birthdays
Grandchildren's Birthdays
Great Grandchildren's Birthdays
Number of Grandchildren
Tire Size
Electric Bill Account
Natural Gas Bill Account
Magazine Subscriptions
Serial Numbers
Television Channels
Film Size
Flight Numbers
Computer Programs
Daily Calorie Counts
Nutritional Counts
Telephone Numbers
Anniversary Date
Voter ID Number

I failed one number test last week when I was asked to fill out my date of death. Not knowing what date I will die, I asked if I could wait until my death occurred. I would then notify them within 3 days after my death if they would approve my credit card application.

I, like everyone else, am being bombarded by these numbers. The only number permitted to exceed the numbers we are required to remember is the amount of the Federal Deficit. Since that number changes by the minute, I just wait to find the amount on the evening news. I sometimes wonder if the Federal Government has conspired to add to the deficit each time we are assigned a new number for some new account we open. I would also venture to say that, one day, we will be requested by the IRS to add up all our account numbers and then write out a check for that amount in order to retire the National Debt.

I am old enough to remember when we were required to count sheep when we were unable to sleep. I have since refrained from counting sheep in fear that they will assign a number to me.

Numbers have also changed my responsibilities and duties as a Househusband. My lists are now numbered. I can no longer be told what jobs to do. I am told to do numbers 3, 5, 5, 5, (3 bathrooms), 8, 10, and 35. I must remember to eat my Basic 4 and Product 9 to maintain my 200 pounds for my 6-foot frame. Keep my calorie intake below 1500, do not take in more than 35mgs cholesterol, and maintain my proper RDA of So3, KCL, and keep my tire pressure at 35lbs psi.

I just remembered that I am on the 2nd floor, there are 19 steps to get downstairs, and that is where I am going to get 3 scoops of ice cream to fill my RDA of junk food. I will do this by the numbers.

Chapter 13

How Not to Surprise Little Wife when She Comes Home

I had it all planned out. I would have everything ready for a surprise for her when she got home. The house was immaculate, by my standards. Dinner was ready. Table set. I had even remembered the napkins.

This was to be a special night. No company, no grandchildren, no great grandchildren. No children, no meetings, nothing good on television, dog fed and pottied. Everything, including the wine, was chilled and the chicken breasts were simmering, salad made. Things could not have been more perfect. I decided the time was right for me to pull off a stunt I had read about recently in the paper. It was some article I had seen about how a wife had prepared things and herself for her spouse when he arrived. Tonight's the night. I was going to emulate that enterprising housewife, but just reverse the roles. I was going all out for her when she arrived.

I got out the material and started my preparations. Tonight was "Plastic Wrap Night." I would do just like the enterprising wife that I had read about and wrap myself in clear plastic food wrap. What a clever idea. Wouldn't she be delighted at my daring and ingenuity? What cleverness on my part to present myself in clinging clear wrap to her when she got home. I just knew that she would be thrilled! Delighted might be a more appropriate term. I could hardly wait for the moment she saw me and how marvelously she would show me how much she appreciated this magnanimous gesture on my part.

I could hardly wait to start. I bathed, shaved, washed my hair, put on my favorite after shave lotion, dashed myself with cologne, and then set about the process of wrapping myself with the clear wrap directly over my freshly bathed skin.

Although it took two rolls of plastic wrap, I felt it was well worth the effort, expense, and excitement. I checked myself in the bathroom full length mirror, made a few adjustments, figured I had very little to work with, so I just accepted things as they were and hoped for the best.

Regular time for her arrival home passed and I was beginning to feel the confinement and sealing properties of the wrap, and began to work up a little sweat. I just figured that the hot, sweaty, uncomfortable feeling would be justified once "My Darling" saw me in her surprise package. I was not concerned about the bulges around the middle, but I did get concerned about the heat being generated and how much I began to sweat inside my package. I tied a big red ribbon around myself and thought I made a beautiful looking present.

I tolerated the discomfort, I sweated out the long wait, and I sat by the window with only a small crack in the blinds. Eventually, the dog let me know that his mother was driving up the driveway.

I was excited, anxious, sweaty, ready to be greeted with the same enthusiasm I felt sure she would have for my efforts. In she came, saying what a hard day she had, how she had trouble at the grocery store, complained about the traffic, hugged the dog, and without looking at her "Surprise Package" barked out commands for me to unload the groceries from the car.

I hurriedly went into the garage and before I could punch the button for the automatic door to close, in walked my neighbor for his evening chat.

There I was. Caught in my own act! Groceries in my arms and me in my wet "Plastic Wrap Sweat Suit!" My enthusiasm vanished while the neighbor howled. He had to call his wife to come witness my "Grocery Carrying Suit" and, by then, I wished I had used aluminum foil so that I could have covered myself and pretended to be "The Tin Man" from "The Wizard of Oz."

No music was necessary since it would have been drowned out by the laughter of the audience: my Darling Wife, my neighbor, and his wife. Even the dog was barking a "laughing bark" at the spectacle turned sour.

When the "fiasco turned sour" was finally over and I had stripped myself of my wrappings, donned my old clothes, and returned to my guests, all I could do was offer them a drink, down several while I was fixing theirs, and return to them to the tune of additional laughter. All I could think about was how well the story would go over at the club tomorrow, all at my expense. No pleading, promises, begging could make them forget the spectacle they had just witnessed.

No amount of prodding, begging or cajoling can make me arrange any further surprises for when my wife comes in from work. I have done my part, failed the course, and will not attempt any further surprises of that nature. I'll just sit back, wait, and watch the dog get all the attention.

Should I try getting down on all fours and wagging my tail when she comes home? I must remember to wear my flea collar.

Chapter 14

Shopping Cart Legislation

Anyone who has ever had the pleasant experience of shopping at a supermarket will have had one or more experiences with the wheeled containers provided shoppers for their convenience while grocery shopping.

While I am not an advocate of additional rules and regulations by "Big Brother," I do feel that the time is just about right for some consumer rights advocate to start the ball rolling on rules, regulations, and laws to regulate the use of these potentially dangerous "people powered" hazards.

One example of the dangers that greet you when you drive into the parking lot of a shopping center is the many empty baskets littering the parking lot. Sure, there are facilities provided to store them until they can be returned to their proper place inside the store, but some parking lot monsters continue to place them in each parking place so that you either park several blocks down the street, or you must get out of your car and move them yourself.

I love the way these carts are returned, eventually, to the inside of the store. They are jammed so tightly together that I think they use a trash compactor! Choosing a cart may just cause you to bust a gut, strain a muscle, or develop a hernia while trying to separate them.

Last week, while I was trying to force several carts apart, some nice lady offered me the use of her pry bar. It worked like a charm. I feel strange sometimes pushing three carts jammed together for my shopping.

Politeness while pushing one of these rolling hazards is "verboten." Nonexistent. Forbidden in polite circles. You have no indication of the intentions of the operators of other carts who stop, turn and block aisle three-way traffic, double and triple-park without benefit of laws, rules or regulations.

Conversations are held in the aisles discussing prices, weather, dress styles, husbands, neighbors, family, soaps, children, bridge games, Boureé games and, all the while, the smaller children are climbing in and out of the baskets adding breakfast food, candy, and other grocery items later found placed on the next handy shelf.

Carts are left unattended, blocking the aisles, while the operators run off to look for items in distant parts of the store. You should see the stares I got when I attempted to move a basket several feet so that I might proceed to the next road blockade. I once spent several hours sandwiched between several seminars while waiting for a chance to get to the next aisle. I was accused by one shopper of hiding her cart while she read the Bible, blocking the aisle. I was pounced upon by the security guard and lectured on the proper way of moving the blocking shopping cart.

I once chose a cart that was actually a new low mileage model, not the depression vintage carts usually found in the stores. This new vehicle actually had 4 wheels that rolled, all in the same direction, and no dents or scratches to mar its beauty. The cart could actually proceed down the aisles without sounding like a Mack truck rolling down the highway on its rims. I was delighted. I shopped all day long just to enjoy the rare occasion of having such supermarket social standing. I tried hiding it in some far off corner just before closing time, but the manager caught me and charged me for excessive use of the cart and not returning it on time.

You could easily distinguish it from the Civil War era carts normally used. The cart had new shiny wheels, well oiled, a clean new handle for pushing, clean baby seat, item locator chart, baby wipes, clean drink holder, and warning lights as your approached congested aisles. I really enjoyed shopping using this cart. Of course, when I finally got to the cashier, reluctant to give up my new cart, I realized I had forgotten my wallet.

Many of these carts disappear from the premises and are used for home delivery, bag people "collectors," and mobile carts for parade vendors, while some are just simply discarded in the nearest drainage ditch. Some stores actually have a licensed, motorized vehicle, usually a large pickup truck called a "Shopping Cart Rescue Vehicle," that patrols the area recovering lost, stolen, or strayed carts.

My wife once noticed patrons using carts for home delivery as they pushed them down the streets of New Orleans. Since we feel that the cost of these shopping carts is part of the cost of items we buy, she resented someone walking off with them, knowing that the price of groceries would rise accordingly, eventually.

She immediately called the police when she arrived home, gave them the location of the carts being pushed and, as required, gave her home address. About 2 hours later, the police did come out, but to our house to inquire about the carts.

What's the use of reporting stolen carts? I think it's time for the DOT (Department of Transportation) to propose legislation governing the use, operation, and licensing of these hazards used to "revictulate."

Among those items to be considered should be:

1. Create schools to teach proper operation of carts while shopping.
2. License all cart operators.
3. Insist that stores and supermarkets maintain enforcement officers on the premises to enforce rules and regulations.
4. Install court facilities for those who violate laws.
5. Forbid double and triple parking in the aisles, reading of labels, visiting, and abandoning shopping carts.
6. Require stores and supermarkets to install clipboards and calculators on each cart, conversion tables figuring ounces to pounds, CCs to pints, pints to gallons, gallons to liters, and kilograms to pounds.
7. Require store operators to lubricate cart wheels every 10,000 miles or every 7 years, whichever comes first.
8. Install soundproof boxes for crying children, patterned after the Pope Mobile.
9. Require renewal of licenses for shopping cart operators every 6 months.
10. Establish a Federal Department to oversee that all laws and regulations governing shopping carts are carried

out, and that each state be mandated to set up proper offices and departments which hire the necessary personnel to operate them.

I intend to forward these rules and regulations to all stores that have shopping carts for use by their customers, as well as all government agencies that will eventually become involved, should these suggestions be adopted.

I feel that with proper government control, the initial layout for expenses involved will cost the government only several million dollars, escalating within a few short years to costing only several billion dollars.

The question is not whether we Househusbands can afford this; it's how long can we survive if we do not get this important legislation passed.

Who knows who the next "Shopping Cart Czar" will be?

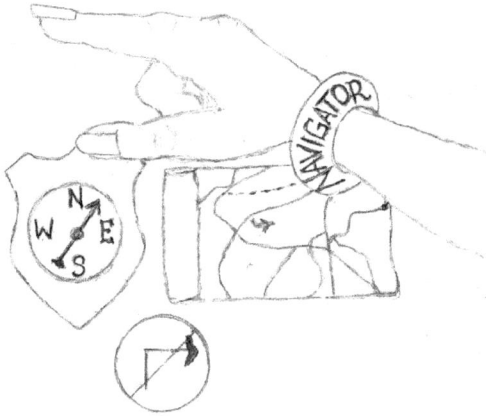

Chapter 15

My Personal Navigator

I feel certain that I can find some survey to confirm the following statistics: 95% of all accidents having husband and wife riding together are caused by the wife telling the husband how to drive; 102% of women passengers will tell the male drivers how to drive; women passengers see potential hazards before they are visible to male drivers; male drivers are always at fault, never the ~~aggravators~~ navigators.

These figures, I'm told, are to be revealed in the first issue of "Househusband International," a men's magazine that should be published weekly. There is a need for this since so many of us fall into this category. The publication will go to press just as soon as Househusbands get permission from their wives.

I look for it every time I am waiting in the checkout line at the supermarket. I have yet to find a copy. I am bombarded with all the trials and tribulations of women in distress but never a tabloid published to help males. We are always the "causer" instead of the "causee." (If I have this backwards, my wife will so inform me.)

Each and every time I drive alone, somewhere from the upholstery there is a voice that warns me, "watch that light, get over in the other lane, you're driving too fast, put both hands on the wheel, I'll change the radio, the car needs vacuuming, and you'd better get some gas, you're almost on half-full." These little sayings must come from the sound bouncing around from the last time the two of us were in the car at the same time.

I once felt that it was a status symbol to have an attractive girl sitting next to me on the front seat, but things changed after marriage. The attractive female became the director, navigator, conductor, adjuster, and chief critic of the family vehicle. She is always the one who tells everyone where to sit, how to get there, what speed to use, what lane to use, adjuster for the radio, temperature, and vents, and a self-appointed critic regarding what I just did that should not have been done, and what I should do next.

This Househusband is always reminded to check to see if the door is properly closed, fasten seat belts, look before backing, adjust the air conditioner, change the radio, answer why I forgot to vacuum the auto carpets, questioned about the umbrella, asked about the hand lotion, questioned about Socrates, and queried about the iron, coffee pot, stove, oven, dishwasher, and telephone answering machine. Once I get over this inquisition, I have forgotten where I am going and how to get to where it is that I forgot I was going.

I was once invited into the cockpit of a 747 to have a look-see around. The crew of the plane had a shorter takeoff checklist than I have when my wife is in the car with me. I can see why the automobile manufacturers have installed lights, bells, buzzers, and hidden voices to remind the driver what to check before moving the vehicle. It was in self-defense. Some wives must have gotten together to insist that they have a backup system to irritate the driver when the wives are not present to do it themselves.

I once had the habit of consulting a map prior to undertaking a trip, either cross town or cross country. However, I soon learned that this was useless since my wife, the navigator, unfolded my map and proceeded to chart a new course for our destination. If things worked out, I would be reminded of the excellent job accomplished. If we got lost, it was always my responsibility to stop and ask directions since my directions were outdated, wrong, and my navigator just knew that we should have turned the opposite way.

I admit to being at fault by not standing my ground when I knew I was right. It has caused us untold wasted hours of trying to get back to where we wanted to go, or getting back to where we came from.

I'll always remember the night, for which I'll take the blame, when we got lost in Mexico City. We were all dressed in coat and tie and Sunday best and on our way to one of the finest restaurants with only seven of our nine children. I plotted out our course before leaving, and then set out for the restaurant. Map in hand, the conductor said that if I would turn on a certain street, I could cut out 2 blocks on a twenty mile trip. I knew better than to argue, but I took the director's advice.

Reservation time came and reservation time went. It continued to get later and later, but we continued the 2 block shortcut. Finally, we were close to the Pyramids north of Mexico City, and we both concurred that we were too far, too late, too tired, too frustrated to continue the pursuit for the evening. Back to our room for crackers and cheese, hang up the good clothes, and wait for another day.

Another day was the next day and we made our reservation time on time, with no shortcuts. Someone realized that the map had been copied in a mirror image, which steered us in exactly the opposite direction from where we intended during our previous attempt.

Another time in Alabama, we were looking for the alternate route of US 98. Simple enough, but simple things very often have a way of becoming complicated at the most inopportune time. I was looking for the alternate sign and, just before I approached the intersection, I was asked if I knew if the Alabama sales tax was 8 or 9 percent. While trying to recall their tax rate, the road sign popped up as Highway 98 and I immediately tried to recall the tax rate, highway number, and maintain control of the car. The only thing I could do was pull off the road, convince my wife that I did not know the tax rate, look at the map again, and try to find US 98 again. I had taken the wrong turn. I do not admit that I made a mistake. I was just trying to remember the proper rate for Alabama's sales tax.

Househusbands are always in the wrong lane. The next lane always moves faster. Never mind that the driver can see miles ahead and has made his choice of lanes; the backseat driver sees several cars pass on the right side and is positive that I should be in the opposite lane. This works directly opposite when driving in a country where the driver sits on the right. I think, in medical terms, the condition is known as "laneaphobia" – the fear of being in the wrong traffic lane and the corresponding desire of changing lanes.

Have you ever wondered why there are so few female auto mechanics? They know too much. Everyone knows that the next problem you have will be the same as Mary Jane had. She had this "grrumbaaaaahuze" sound, took it down to the repair shop, and was told it was the transmission. My wifey had a new sound in her car, brought it in, and told the service representative that she had the same sound that Mary Jane had. She just knew it was the transmission. Upon inspection, the transmission was still attached to the car, but a tree limb was caught in the frame and was dragging along the street causing the new noise. Seven months later, the brake shoes started squeaking so she had the transmission checked again. I hope Mary Jane hears about this so she can have the same trouble.

A short 4-block trip can produce the following one-sided conversation:

"Honey, make sure your doors are locked."

I did.

"Did you lock the doors?"

I did.

"Be sure to turn on your headlights."

I did.

"Turn down the air conditioner."

I do.

"Change the radio to another station."

I do.

"Be sure to stop at the corner."

I did.

"Don't turn so fast."

I did not.

"Adjust your rearview mirror."

I did.

"Check to make sure you can see out the side view mirrors."

I did.

"Watch out for that light."

I did.

"Look out for that car."

I did.

"Watch out for that child on the bike."

I did.

"Turn here; this is the street we want."

I did.

"Park on the right side."

I did.

"Pull up a little bit."

I did.

"Unlock the door."

I did.

"Be sure to lock the doors."

I did.

"Did you lock the doors?"

I did and proceeded to make some comment.

I am immediately cut short by the conductor, director, navigator, and critic with her remark, "You irritate me. You think you know it all."

We now have a new device called a "GPS" that gives us complete directions. If they are right, we arrive at our planned destination. If not, then we can both blame it on the GPS.

Chapter 16

Bridge

Every Friday night about 6PM, the preparations begin for an evening that will produce unpredictable results. The outcome is too early to predict since the action has not yet taken place. This is the time when clothes are checked, baths are taken, last minute strategies are discussed, and the finger food is arranged for all the evening guests. All necessary preparations have been completed, tables arranged, chairs are set out at the tables, cards are spread out, pencils sharpened, and score pads are out on the tables.

At exactly 7PM, the doorbell starts ringing and the participants begin to arrive. Purses and coats are taken, fees are paid, tallies (score cards/name cards) distributed, and a quick exchange of the week's activities discussed. Pat and Rob, Blanche and Don, Jackie and Bob, and Wife and I are the participants for tonight's game. Larry and Lynette have moved to Houston, so they are invited to substitute when they are in town. The names are not their real names to protect the guilty.

Only those who play the game of bridge can appreciate the rules, regulations, and conventions of the game. The conventions vary from city to city. Only a dedicated fan of the game can follow and appreciate the conventions, rules, and bidding that the players are given. Whoever gets the highest scores by the end of the evening wins the money.

Each player is given a number and the numbers are paired off with a second number held by each player's partner. That is how the partners are assigned. Four players make up a table. Tonight we have 2 tables, eight players. Each player grabs a quick cup of coffee or drink and returns to the table that matches his tally. Table one is always the closest to the kitchen.

Now the fun begins, the arguments start, and spouses begin to give their instructions to their spouses on how the bid should go, or should have gone, and complaints are registered by those who receive unbiddable hands.

Tonight, the first set of partners consists of husband and wife and, as they are seated and last minute instructions are issued, the cards are dealt, 13 to each player. Rob draws the high card, so he is the dealer. He deals, then arranges his hand, counts his points, and opens 1 diamond. My hand contains only 7 points, so I pass and don't make a bid. Pat looks into her hand and counts her points, likes what she sees, and bids 2 no trump. My wife frowns at me and passes. Rob gets to bid again, quickly adding his points to Pat's bid, and determines that they, together, can arrive at a bid that will give them the necessary points for a game. He bids 5 diamonds, which would give them a game.

I lead off and Pat proceeds to put her hand down, since she is the dummy. Now the fun begins. Rob studies the table and tells everyone that he will make 7 tricks and that Pat has grossly underbid. Pat insists that today's newspaper had this hand and that this was the proper bid. My wife tells me that I should have given a bid of something other than a pass. Pat continues to discuss their bid and they, eventually, end up with the necessary tricks to complete their game contract.

After the hand is played, more discussions take place and the hand is "replayed" while all examples are given as to what would have taken place if I had led a certain card, and if my wife would have trumped my card earlier in the game. If my wife had had more points, and I would have responded to her, then we could have taken an additional trick and we could have set them 2 tricks.

Now, I realize that a discussion can lead to being a better player, but when someone waits to ask a question while all the other discussions are taking place, you usually forget what question you would have asked if you had only gotten the chance. Oh, well! Next time, you will be first to ask the question and your question will probably be discussed first. But, don't count on it.

I almost forgot that table 2 was playing in the other room. Don is the dealer and Blanche is his partner. Bob and Jackie are partners at that table. Don deals and opens with one club. Jackie is sitting with enough points to respond with a preempt bid of 3 hearts. Blanche passes and Don does not have enough points to continue bidding, so Jackie receives the bid for 3 hearts. She then proceeds to ask Bob why he passed her 3 hearts bid and Bob starts to defend his choice by explaining why as he lays down his hand. She begins to tell him what he should have bid, how he should have bid, and that she never leaves him in such a bid without arriving at a different contract.

Husbands should, by now, know exactly what their wives had in mind. After all, they have been married for so long that they should know what their wives are thinking.

Now this continues with different episodes and contracts being made, bad bidding, discussions, bad plays and, surprisingly, some good hands being played as the evening progresses. Eventually, all players do get new partners and their game improves with their new partners. Their new partners are too polite to point out their partner's shortcomings.

The evening progresses, stories continue, and food and drinks are consumed and, eventually, all scores are brought together to see who will receive the highest score for the evening. Regardless of how the score cards and partners come out, thank goodness our goodnights are made and discussions follow deciding who will host the game next week.

Bridge is a funny game. You fuss over the cards you receive, glory or growl at the partner's response, and repeatedly return for more of the same at the first invitation to play again.

I am not exactly sure why I continue to try to play at this game. Is it for the company, food, fun, or do I just hope that someday I will learn the game? Maybe it's none of the above. Maybe I just enjoy the confusion that goes with the game.

One bit of advice that I have observed since I started the game is this: a married couple that plays cards together is just an argument that has not yet started. The discussions and corrections will continue on the drive home.

Chapter 17

But You'd Make a Wonderful Santa

My services were committed before I knew what I was committed to. I was volunteered without volunteering. Sergeant Wife had agreed that I would be Santa Claus for her ladies club, even before I knew anything about it.

I know that I'm about the right size. I am told that daily. However, I do not have a beard, my hair is gray, not white, and I have a French accent when I say, "Heaux, Heaux, Heaux." I am jolly at times, at other times I am like a Buddha, all mime and mass. I have been known to make noise, and many of my friends look at me and say, "Pass the bread, here comes the baloney."

I get very nervous when I get around a bunch of women, and I am very shy in their presence. I can hardly speak to a group of more than two and want to run away from crowds of three or more. I get tongue-tied and can only stand around and listen to the jabbering when in the presence of females. In short, I am really a shy person.

How should I act as a Santa? I am assured that all I will have to do is sit around and hand out candy to the ladies as they come in. I will not have to say anything, do anything, or act in any way or capacity other than being my normal self. Little did I know what I had been volunteered for.

I was furnished one of those "fit-all" Santa suits that would have been a perfect fit for Paul Bunyan. There are no pockets for anything, leggings to put over my shoes, a floppy cap to wear, and no beard. How could I possibly expose myself to sixty women without a beard? A frantic call to a frantic chairperson produced a beard on short order. I was furnished a mop that had been bleached. Not just an ordinary mop, but the industrial type that weighed in the neighborhood of twenty pounds.

If it was supposed to pull my head down in a stooped position, it did a remarkable job. My chin rested on my chest, but my neck muscles were strengthened as I constantly raised my head to see who was next in line to be greeted.

I was not allowed to enter into the sacred halls of the gathering place, but was forced to remain on the outside like some uninvited guest. The food was on the inside, out of my reach. Mounds of "Christmas Finger Food" were heaped high upon the table, testing its load design by the weight of the prepared dishes. I was discriminated against by being forced to remain on the outside. The house had no chimney, so I did not know how to enter.

I was never prepared for the onslaught of females or what their actions would be when they met Santa. They wanted to sit on my lap, kiss my cheek and, in plain language, make my life miserable. I suffered through all this, posing for pictures, giving out candy to the ladies, suffering each time there was a new arrival. I was at the point of exhaustion and wondered how long I would have to endure such attacks by members of the opposite sex. I knew they were the opposite sex since I was the only member of my sex present.

My legs ached from the weight of the women who just had to sit on my lap. My arms suffered from being forced to hold them tight so that they would not fall off. My cheeks were red. I thought I was bleeding. I had been photographed, pinched, sat on, hugged, kissed, squeezed, and requested to bring them presents for Christmas. They all told me that they had been good little girls.

I was weak from the constant force I had to exert to hug all of them. I was embarrassed by all the attention being focused on me by members of the opposite sex. I longed to change into comfortable clothes, get rid of my twenty pound mop beard, and get at the food. I was weak and needed nourishment.

Finally, after several hours of torture, pain, anguish, suffering, and distress, I was rescued from this wild group of "Santa Molesters" and brought into the inner halls to partake in the remaining food. I managed to get the two remaining finger sandwiches, one glass of punch, two carrot sticks, one celery stick, no dip, and one small morsel of "Gateau." I felt that I was totally neglected in my "Santa" role, but I was exhausted, tired, depleted, wearied, fatigued, worn out, and completely debilitated. I was almost too exhausted to drive home. I sat in the car, too weak to turn on the ignition. I tried to summon up the strength to drive home. Slowly, I began to start the car, select the proper gear, slowly creep home, barely able to haul myself into the house.

Once inside, I sat myself down near the telephone, looked up the number of the chairperson, and enthusiastically begged for the same job next year.

Chapter 18

What! Me Buy Girdles?

As a Househusband, I can never envision what the next job request will be. I can only wait to hear what the, "Dear, would you please" supplication will be requested of me. I must say that my wife is very polite. She always calls me "Dear" when asking for something.

On one occasion, before I realized it, I had agreed to go downtown and purchase girdles for my little wife. It was on my list before I came to my senses. Once the list is made, my wife considers it cast in stone. I can never change, modify, alter, subtract, or add to the list anything that I cannot expect to accomplish.

The assignment was presented to me in such a manner that I knew I would have no trouble once I found the proper store and department. Little did I realize that I would experience a day in my life that I would remember for all eternity.

I had wanted to acquaint myself with the marvels of public transportation for many months, so I decided that two experiences in one day was just the thing for me to do. I did not realize the workings of the New Orleans Public Transportation System, better known as the RTA, could so thoroughly, so absolutely, so unconditionally confuse someone into thinking they had been hijacked and transported through the maze of a human zoo, or outer space.

I am a person who has many personal policies or hang-ups. Some good, some very eccentric, and others downright void of common sense. One of those policies dictates that I always have something to read, once there is the remote possibility that I might be required to sit or stand for long or short periods of time. I consider this one of my finer qualities.

The pain, discomfort, and anguish of shopping have convinced me that I should never go shopping without a book. I had only a short two block walk to the bus stop but, once at the bus stop, I again realized the wisdom of having a book to get into while waiting for the RTA. After a considerable wait, and then waiting a little longer, I, eventually, viewed the approach of a bus in the distance. The bus stopped, I boarded, and we proceeded to take off like the start of the Indy 500.

After recovering my equilibrium, it was then I was informed that I must have the correct change. The driver would not change my five dollar bill. You guessed it! No change! My pockets were completely void of coins of any size, denomination, or quality. Some kind soul reinstated my faith in humanity and changed my five dollar bill and I was all set for the trip downtown and the maze of routes taken by the bus line.

After considerable detours into parts of town I never knew existed, we finally arrived at the Central Business District (CBD). Of course, the bus stop was some considerable distance from the girdle department store. Not realizing that I could have gotten a transfer, I decided to walk. I also did not know which bus to take, and I did not want to show my ignorance by asking and possibly having to tell someone that I had to buy girdles for my wife.

I started walking the several blocks to the girdle store. The lunch counter of an establishment along the way beckoned to me and I yielded to the temptation of its alluring call. I was convinced that coffee was all I wanted until my counter mate had a Danish placed within my eyesight. Then, it was off to the races and I knew that I needed the fortification of my own personal Cream Cheese Danish. Consuming the calorie/cholesterol mortal sin, I then decided to get in a few pages of my book prior to the "girdle safari."

After an hour sitting with one hand on the coffee cup and the other hand on the book, I was gently asked by the manager to relinquish my seat to someone who was willing to further advance the required cash sales that most businesses find necessary for a successful future.

The manager was very nice and offered me a chance to sit and read in the shoe department while I waited for my wife. I thanked him and informed him that I was alone and that I must leave and proceed to purchase girdles for my wife. I couldn't understand why he had such a confused look on his face. He looked at me in complete bewilderment as I closed my book and walked out of his store.

Realizing that it was time to make the final push to carry out my main assigned task for the day, I set my book under my arm, squared off my shoulders, convinced my feet that they must carry me to the girdle store, and pushed forward. Now I know how General Eisenhower felt when he had to make the final decision for the Normandy invasion on "D-Day."

My determination was dampened once I was inside the girdle store and became aware that it was sale day. Every woman in New Orleans, except my wife, had left their chores for the day to attend this sale. I sought out a clerk who seemed to be the "milquetoast" type and asked for directions to the girdle department.

Well, she did not know exactly where the girdle department was located, but with all the determination and volume of the winner of the hog calling contest at the State Fair, and the volume of a Lyric Mezzo Soprano hitting the highest note possible, she yelled out the following to no one in particular: "This man wants to know where the girdle department is located." All heads turned to see just who had the "ships horn" type of voice. I conveniently dropped my book, bent down to pick it up, and tried to avoid the stares of the female population of New Orleans, less one.

The clerk with the "ships horn voice" finally found me under the counter and directed me to the lingerie floor. As I climbed the stairs, I could feel all heads turn, except one, mine, to watch the man who was in the store just to find the girdle department.

Three more clerks later, I found myself among the most squealing bunch of females I have ever seen or heard. They were grabbing, shoving, pulling, throwing; looking for the proper size, color, and shade; trying on the items; and chasing loose children. I figured I knew nothing about shopping and started to leave when some kind elderly lady asked if she could help. I thankfully accepted her offer and told her that I would like to purchase some girdles, forgetting to add that they were for my wife.

This prompted her to spring into action and, within seconds, the manager and three security guards had me boxed in like a quarterback for the Saints trying to pass the ball for the winning touchdown. All of the female population of New Orleans, less one, was trying to get at this man, me, calling me the sex pervert of the century. After I finally convinced them that my one and only purpose was to purchase girdles for my wife, the manager and his three stooges, KGB-type agents stood by me to make sure I purchased the items, paid for them, and then saw to it that I had safe passage to the store exit.

I now had the attention of the proper girdle clerk who proceeded to ask me the size. Then, she asked for the color. Next, the shade. The style. Then, the material – cotton or nylon? The guards looked at me quizzically when I was able to produce only part of the necessary information. I then made a mental note to make sure that I had a note and permission slip ready if ever I was called upon to perform such a task again.

I glanced around and pointed to one woman who was approximately the size of my wife and indicated that my wife was about the same size as that lady over there. I later found out that this could be construed as actual sexual harassment and that I was not allowed to make such remarks in public. My offer to try the girdles on for size was met with a frown, scowl, jeers, and a warning that any further remarks would have to be explained in the presence of a judge in the courtroom.

I was informed that the colors were white, pink, flesh, nude, brown, black, blue, and blush. I thought that the clerk was telling me to blush, so I did a masterful job of it. I mentioned the color nude and again was subjected to the fourth degree by Mr. Manager and the three KGB-type agents. I finally resorted to pointing to the proper color, making sure that I blushed red, turned blue, and felt like I was yellow. I finally found my permission slip, and the necessary information in my pocket, and made my purchase. I paid for my purchases, and the procession of Mr. Manager and the three KGB-type strong arm agents kept their promise. I was escorted down the stairs, package in hand, past the "ships horn voice" clerk to the main entrance. But, not before the "ships horn voice" female clerk got in her final blow wanting to know if I had found my girdles!

By then, I was again on the receiving end of the staring eyes of the entire female population of New Orleans, less one, all straining to see the man who had purchased the girdles. And, at this point, I was totally and absolutely humiliated beyond belief.

I was wet with sweat, but did not dare remove any article of clothing for relief, afraid that I might be charged with public nudity. I felt that the security guards had informed the NOPD that there was some weirdo on the loose and that they'd better put out an APB on him for possible trouble.

I made another fatal mistake. This was my day for mistakes. I put my book in my bag and a quick glance over my shoulder convinced me that I was not being followed by the vice squad of the NOPD, Mr. Manager, the KGB-type agents, and the entire female population of New Orleans, less one.

By this time, I felt like I was dehydrated and badly needed a drink, so I convinced myself that the fortification of a powerful libation would restore my confidence for the return trip home. Drink ordered, my purchase on the counter, I was all set to relax and congratulate myself for surviving the entire ordeal when, just down the bar, someone overturned their drink and my shopping bag seemed to soak up the entire contents of the spilled drink.

Wet sack in hand, unfinished drink on the bar, I stormed out of the place and sought refuge at a quick lunch counter before hunting for the bus stop. By now, I was convinced that there was either a Communist or Croatian plot against me. My shopping bag had been rendered useless by the spilled drink. I was forced to balance six exposed boxes of girdles, three nude in color, and one soggy, wet paperback in my open arms, while waiting my turn in line to get a seat at the lunch counter.

The manager of the lunch counter warned me that counter space was limited, so would I please limit myself to being served, then eat, pay, and leave.

Suffice to say that the conversation matched the eyes staring at my predicament and it, eventually, evolved into questions and jeers from the audience regarding my purchases piled high on the counter next to my sandwich.

At this point in time, I wondered, could my darling wife possibly have known just how this would all turn out? I would have, at this point, welcomed a phone call from the lady trying to sell me house siding, just to assure me that someone would talk to me about something else other than girdles.

By that time, I had had enough frustration for one day. I was red with embarrassment, wet with sweat, smelly with spilled drink, and no one would bid me the time of day, much less help with directions to the proper bus stop. A friendly policeman finally gave me the information, but only after warning me that he would run me in if I caused any trouble. I was beginning to feel that being hauled in would have been a relief. Then, I could call my wife and she would come and either bail me out and take me home, or I would be confined to the comfort of some jail cell.

After an hour of balancing my girdles, standing, and reading my soggy book, the bus came and I, of course, dropped my girdles while reaching for my bus fare. Girdles retrieved, I concentrated on finding a seat. School had just been let out and the bus was full of school children and sale day shopping ladies, less one. This necessitated me having to stand, trying to balance book and girdles, while hanging on for dear life and attempting to spare myself even more embarrassment.

I now know what it feels like to be ridiculed in public. The students never did let up on me, the man with the nude girdles. The steam being emitted from all of the sweat glands of my body prevented any of these remarks from being retained for later memory. Otherwise, they would have filled a book telling others how to humiliate a girdle-toting smelly husband while riding a bus.

Lo and behold, the next stop was actually mine. I released the grip on the overhead bar to pull the cord to stop the bus. You guessed it! Down went the girdles and book, as I felt one last blow to the only remaining thread of dignity I felt I possessed. The other passengers were most helpful in making sure I had all my girdles, and my wet, soggy book on the stack of girdles, when I left the confines of the bus. I figured that, by now, I was home free. Just several blocks to walk and I would be within the safety of my home. There I could relax, put down my burden, fix a drink, enjoy a shower, change into clean clothes, and just wait for approval of my purchases.

Wrong! Wrong! Wrong! It seemed like all the ladies in the subdivision, less one, were out for a stroll in the afternoon sun. I did my best to answer their questions about my purchases, nude in color, and demonstrate courtesies to my neighbors, but, somehow, it was just not meant to be. I was yellow turning red.

I finally made it to the sanctuary of my home and did as I had planned to do. I relaxed, bathed, changed clothes, and was just beginning to relax with a homemade drink, when in walked the "woman of the house" accusing me of goofing off all day while she was off in the "work war zone."

No explanation of my day was satisfactory to her. I was making it all up. I just wanted her sympathy. I presented my purchases to the little woman. I just knew that after washing, the offensive odor would be eliminated from the nude girdles. I ate my dinner in total and complete silence. I changed the paper on the dog's tray and then waited for some hint of approval for my day.

I finally got my reward for the harrowing day I had experienced. Heading the list for tomorrow, I read, "Honey, would you please go downtown and exchange these girdles for a larger size?"

Chapter 19

I Get PMS

For years now, I have been hearing about PMS. I was too bashful to ask just what it meant. I finally decided that it meant "Positive Masculine Syndrome." I labored under this misconception for years until I heard women comment that they, too, had PMS.

I began to understand that it must be something other than my original idea of its meaning. I realized that only the masculine sex could not have it since women continued to express "their" condition as suffering from PMS.

I continued to live in ignorance of the malady and finally concluded that Househusbands could also get the dreaded PMS on a routine basis. I am convinced that anyone, male or female, husband or wife, rich or poor, can and do get the "monthlies" on a regular basis.

I am working with a friend who is a statistician and seems to support my theory that all households, at some time, experience the pains on a regular basis. No one is immune to PMS; however, certain occupations seem to have encountered PMS more frequently than others.

Never having been a housewife, I am not qualified to speak for them. Their symptoms are similar. I am, however, qualified as a Househusband to speak for my fraternal brothers.

PMS is the disease brought about by the Househusband having to remain around the house to carry on the burden of household duties. Once I accomplish my household tasks, I usually revert to the reclusive stage and wallow in the torments of PMS. I have done my duties of mopping, dusting, cleaning, washing, repairing, mowing, weeding, painting, shopping, fixing, answering, waiting, sorting, cooking, baking, caring for dog, and a host of other duties. This is the time I reflect on my accomplishments and suffer through the hard times brought on by PMS.

I look for sympathy from my wife. I find none. I turn to the dog; I find none. I call my friends; I get no sympathy. I watch the soaps; I get more pains. My PMS continues to get more severe.

I look around the house, the yard, the garage. All I find is more and more to do, although I have less and less energy at my disposal, or the corresponding desire to accomplish my assigned tasks. I fight to maintain my balance between inside chores and outside chores. The demands of the inside are more demanding than the outside.

I keep dreaming that Socrates will learn how to put all of his energies to good use and take over the outside chores. I keep on dreaming. He keeps on playing.

I maintain a constant battle with my list. I scratch off jobs, yet they somehow reappear. The list continues to grow until I feel that the more calories I consume, the longer the list grows. The bigger the list gets, the larger I get in size. I realize I am a victim of the system. I am a Househusband whose work never gets done; I have an ever-growing list of jobs and recurring cases of PMS.

I visit my family doctor. He finds nothing wrong with me. He says I should find more things to keep me busy. I visit my psychiatrist and he assures me it's nothing to worry about. I wonder if I should have a hysterectomy or maybe a mammogram.

I will shortly overcome my symptoms. He scoffs at the idea that I have PMS and tells me to forget about it. Go out and find some volunteer work to perform.

I continue my normal routine. I "fight" my list of chores and the symptoms. I dare not discuss it with anyone. My wife suspects something but cannot put her finger on the problem.

I discuss it with her and put all my cards on the table. She thinks I should take bridge lessons. I convince her that something is wrong with me and she finally agrees with me.

Only thing is, she refers to my PMS as the "Poor Me Syndrome."

Chapter 20

Work Until It's Done

The person who first uttered the saying, "A woman's work is never done" was a person who had very little vision or knowledge. They left themselves wide open for a rebuttal. It is very obvious that the person who said it knew nothing of a Househusband.

If a woman's work is never done, how can the Househusband ever finish his work and a woman's work?

I will be one of the first to agree that housework is never done. Things might be clean and presentable around the house, but there is always something to do once a job is finished. The outside of a house requires just as much attention as the inside. Once I finish the front yard, the back yard needs attention.

I have attempted to have yard and house in order to the point that the "Inspector General" would walk in, look around, and give me an "A" for having everything finished. Never once has this goal become a reality either to her satisfaction or mine. There is always something waiting to be done.

If I have cleaned the floors, mopped, waxed, buffed, vacuumed rugs, and passed a white cloth just before the "General" arrives, I can be sure that she will find grit on the floor and proceed to either sweep or vacuum before saying hello to either Socrates or Househusband.

There is always another counter to be wiped, an item of clothing to be picked up, clothes to be folded, weeds to be pulled, clothes to be ironed, items to be painted, grass to be cut, dishes to be washed, trees and shrubs to be trimmed, garbage to be taken out, cars to be vacuumed, furniture to be dusted, letters to be answered, things to be put away, and phone calls to be answered, bills to be paid, and shopping to be done. All this must be done after walking the dog.

I am in full agreement with the saying about her work never being done, but I am fully aware that this Househusband will never be able to "get done" all the work desired or required of himself. I have become paranoid from trying to guess which task is most important each day. I try to accomplish the most important jobs only to find out that taping the soaps is more important than changing the oil in the car. Having the bridge tables set up for her party is more important than my golf game. Socrates should be walked before I try to read my paper.

I have contemplated forming a Househusbands Union to combat this feeling that my work is never done, but I gave up the idea when Wife insisted that this Union be opened to female membership. I know the Supreme Court would side with women on this issue so I backed down. I was permitted to form my own Union of two, with the deciding vote going to, guess who?

The next time I hear the saying, "A man's work is from sun to sun but a woman's work is never done," you can bet I'll have a ready answer.

My house was cleaned last month, sorry you missed it.

Chapter 21

Time to Say Goodbye

We knew it was bound to happen, sooner or later. After seventeen years, Socrates, her dog, could no longer run and jump and play.

He was a loyal member of the family and was diligent in performing his duties as a member of the family, albeit as dog. Soc loved his family and the grandchildren, and met family and friends with greetings that matched his adopted Mother and Father.

For those of us who enjoy sharing our lives with our pets, parting with them brings a sadness that remains for long periods of time.

Eventually, we sought to fill in the gap by adopting a new pet. This is not an easy task, and the choice came about rather suddenly.

We were suddenly offered a chance to adopt an Australian Shepherd, not a miniature, but one that would very likely get to be about fifty or sixty pounds.

Our bedroom could be considered oversized, so that meant rearranging the furniture to accommodate the new arrival, Patches. Naturally, Househusband occupied the exact space that Patches needed for his comfort. Dog beds – yes, dog beds – had to be provided, a toy box had to be supplied, pillows were needed, blankets for his beds, and other non-necessities for his comfort.

I was very agreeable to give up my comforts, especially since I thought that I would be provided with new pillow, blanket, a better position for TV viewing, and a better chance for a place to sit and enjoy the rare benefit of affection from my wife.

Not so. Patches occupies a bed located between us, with his head facing away from me. His other end is pointed in my direction. My recliner cannot be reclined since Patches might be in a position to be crushed should I ever again be allowed to enjoy the reclining position of my easy chair.

Since I am closer to the door to the outside, it always seems to be more convenient for me to get up and let Patches out for certain bodily functions. Once he finishes his business, I am the only one that he calls on to return to his position between our chairs.

Patches is not all bad. He always indicates that he wants to go outside, play ball, go for walks, or just remind me that he wants attention of some kind. He gets his nose under my arm and keeps raising it in a jerky motion to let me know that it is time for something to happen. His favorite time to nose me under the arm is when I try to sneak in a nap or just when I start on some task. He has a sixth sense of how and when to disturb me.

His manners are impeccable. Patches will not snitch food off the counter. I am positive my wife has trained him to come running once he hears the sound of the cookie jar being raided or the unwrapping of a slice of cheese. He is very loyal about informing my wife when I deviate from my diet. He usually does not tell when I cheat between meals unless I refuse to share with him.

Patches is good company, sometimes a nuisance, inquisitive, loyal, well-trained, friendly, clean, handsome, well-mannered, and a joy to have around most of the time. When he wags his short tale, it reminds me of helicopter blades swirling. He loves visitors, children, walks, whatever you're eating, and he's always ready to jump in the car for a ride or play ball. He understands certain phrases in English, French, Italian, and Spanish.

Maybe in his old age, Patches will respect my old age and allow me to regain my status in my own home.

Chapter 22

Honey, Would You Fix Dinner?

This is not a request, a command, nor is it a suggestion; it's actually all three, with additional instructions to come.

Naturally, I agree to do it. I will have completed tomorrow's list in plenty of time to comply. What I do not realize is that there are additional instructions on what to fix, how to fix it, when to fix it, and how much to fix.

I write down the instructions the night before and place them in a safe place so that I can find them in the morning. Just to make sure I do find them, I attach them to my "news watching chair" by my Darling's chair. That way, I can't miss them in the morning.

After re-consulting the list, I figure that I should start dinner preparations at 10AM so that all dishes come together at 6PM.

Directions are to defrost the ground meat for the meatloaf. Use very little salt, no black pepper, just lemon pepper, do not add bread crumbs, use the onions in the pantry that are getting old, chop up the bell pepper in the refrigerator, add some herbs from the garden, add one cup of wheat germ, mix the contents together, and form into a loaf. Pour a can of tomato soup over the loaf in the baking pan, and then bake in the oven at 350º until done. Additional instructions follow but, while I am getting the necessary ingredients together, my list falls from the cabinet.

I look for the list for the next forty-five minutes, and then I realize that Patches has found it before I did and thought it would substitute for chewing gum. By the time I retrieve it from Patches, the list is just a wad of wet paper that might just as well have been written in Chinese. It's useless.

I start to prepare the meatloaf as I think I remember the instructions. I finally get the meat defrosted after using the ice pick, forks, knives, food processor, hair dryer, salt, and crying and begging from Patches. I mop the floor to remove flying debris from my difficult defrosting process and return to my duties.

None of the ingredients are where they are supposed to be. The bell pepper is in the freezer, the onions were used up last week, oatmeal is used instead of wheat germ, and I am out of salt.

No dinner preparations can be made without at least one trip to the supermarket. I probably will forget what it is that I'm going for, but I set out to purchase the missing ingredients anyway.

I return to the scene and continue to prepare my meatloaf. The ingredients are finally combined, with all of the confusion possible, and the contents are placed in the oven. The oven is carefully set and the door is closed.

The phone rings. The estimator from the siding company will be in my neighborhood tomorrow and would like to give me a price for siding on my home. I muster up my most mellifluous voice and politely decline the offer.

An hour later, I peek at the meatloaf only to realize that the oven was properly set but not turned on. I figure that if I raise the temperature, it will cook faster and be ready when "Honey Bun" arrives.

I experience a sense of euphoria at my ingenuity and proceed to see about a vegetable. I like carrots and peas, so I settle on the yellow and green combination of the two. I know now that I should have peeled the carrots before putting them into the microwave. I also know that it takes considerably less than forty-five minutes to microwave the peas and carrots.

I almost forget the salad, so I chop the lettuce, slice the tomatoes, and add the artichoke hearts. In my mind, it is a masterpiece.

I discover then that we are out of salad dressing, so this necessitates another journey to the supermarket. I better get another bottle of wine just to make sure we have enough.

I return home with my purchases. All of a sudden, it occurs to me that I did not check on the fat content of the foods I was trying to prepare. I quickly look at the meat, peek in on the carrots and peas, admire my salad, and determine that I am safe on all counts and that I should forge on ahead with the job at hand. Things are completely under control.

I set the table putting the knife and spoon on the right side, the small fork and the dinner fork on the left side, set out matching dishes, forget the napkins, pour the milk, fill the wine glasses, and set the candles at ready. All I need now is for my wife to breeze in, pay attention to the dog, and plant herself at the table waiting for the feast.

Today is the day that my "Olympic Shopping Champion" decides to indulge in a marathon spree so my dinner sits waiting for the next two hours. Finally, the garage door opens, in walks the champion shopper, arms laden with packages. She had hit a sale and found some really fantastic bargains. She even bought me a present! With a great deal of fanfare and explanation, she hands me my gift. I expect a new ring, or watch, or tie tack, or a dozen golf balls. I am extremely excited about opening my present. I am extremely disappointed to discover that I am the new owner of six new dish towels. I'll bet this goes over big at the Friday night bridge game.

I pour the wine and start to set the dishes on the table. The salad is limp like a wet paper towel. The peas are hard like buckshot. The carrots are hard enough to be used as darts, and the meatloaf is as close to being cremated as only a novice, such as I, could have made it. The wine is excellent. So is the second glass.

By the third glass, I have lost all interest in the meal, have had my ears filled with the proper method of food preparation, and must clean the kitchen before going out to the local restaurant for a proper meal.

I really believe that now my wife enjoys cooking on the weekend so that we might have food prepared for the entire next week.

Chapter 23

It's All a Hoax

The time came when my title as "Househusband" changed to the dubious title of husband again. I did not relinquish the duties, only the chance to perform at my own rate of speed, and title of master of my house from 7AM to 5PM.

My wife retired again, and again resumed command of the household. I was happy to turn over the position to her but was reluctant to forfeit my feeling of independence and choices of relaxation times.

I had begun to fancy myself as a writer during my time as Househusband and had written several potentially dangerous chapters for this manuscript. I had also convinced myself that someday I would attempt to make sense of the previously written chapters.

Recently, I made the unfortunate mistake of leaving this manuscript within reach and guess who found it? That's right. My Darling Wife found it. I had meant to keep this a secret from her, knowing full well that she would never approve its contents. I hid it in the back of my computer with a secret code so that she could not possibly pull it up on the screen.

Actually, she never found the file on the computer. She found the copy of this manuscript that I had printed. That was my undoing.

After my wife finished reading the contents, while gradually reaching her boiling point, she summoned me into the inner chambers of our home and, there on the carpet, she demanded a full explanation of just what I meant by writing such a mixed up jumble of words, full of untruths. What would her friends think of her should anyone ever find out about my writings about her?! She demanded an immediate retraction of all derogatory words, passages, phrases, references, and innuendos.

She then demanded that I leave off this chapter, rewrite it, or simply just tell the truth. After months of cogitating, thought, considering, and verbal instructions, my wife finally consented to the following.

My wife is really a lovely person. She is kind, gentle, beautiful, sympathetic, understanding, generous, loving, and open-minded. She has consistently made a home for me and our children, has filled our home with wall-to-wall love, and has been like a fruitful vine, a beacon, who constantly is giving of herself, her love, her encouragement, her wit, her humor, her guidance, her direction, and her constant companionship.

She has been a beacon of light on our journey, a constant reminder of all that I could have ever asked for or desired in a wife, a mother, a sweetheart, a companion, and a friend.

She has never once raised her voice to me in any manner that would suggest that she has ever had the slightest displeasure with any of my actions or opinions during our 51 years of marriage. She has always complimented me, encouraged me, and approved of what I do or what I have done. She has given me free reign with my ideas and opinions, and has never uttered any type of criticism of anything I have ever done.

She loves me and I love her. She could never do anything that I would not consider as perfect. She is, has always been, and will always be the most perfect wife that any Househusband could ever ask for.

Editor's note: This last chapter was dictated to the author, and his wife insisted that it be included in this unauthorized manuscript.

My Wife

When God joined man and wife,
He failed to realize there might be strife.
He made man and gave him free will,
He never intended that husbands be pills,
But husbands would never be still.

He made man in his image and likeness,
He told them to go forth and find kindness.
Man looked for instructions and soon realized
That help was needed
For he and his friends to survive.

They looked all around and they soon found
What they were seeking was lurking around.
God had provided creatures abound.
He called them women, for he liked the sound.
God fed them and clothed them in Nature's own way,
And soon men and women were well on their way.

These two creatures would soon realize
That they needed more if they were to survive.
They discussed it with each other,
Let nature take its course,
And soon realized there was more to discover.

Man soon realized how important it was,
The comforting feeling to have one another.
His new companion was given the name,
And with that act, things were never the same.
His new companion was now called "Wife"
Then became "Mother" adding joy to his life.

Now all the world has a Mother,
And some men have a wife.
Let us all realize what it would be like
For man to survive without a wife.

Man continues to battle with strife,
But now has help along with his wife.
To face unafraid the life he has made,
With love and affection,
The fruit of his selection,
A wife to help in his quest for direction.

C. Earl Weber I

AUTHOR'S NOTE

The author presently resides in Lafayette, Louisiana, with his wife, and several of his children, grandchildren and great grandchildren live nearby. His time is spent writing about his family history, life experiences, the grandchildren, traveling and other interests and favorite subjects. He and his wife also spend time at his camp on the Atchafalaya River.

The author may be contacted at Epawgram@aol.com.